MASTERING
HIGH NET
WORTH
SELLING

The Critical Path

MASTERING
HIGH NET
WORTH
SELLING

The Critical Path

**Your CRITICAL PATH to
Building a Successful
21st Century
Financial Practice**

Matt Oechsli

TOTAL ACHIEVEMENT PUBLISHING · GREENSBORO, NORTH CAROLINA

Other books by Matt Oechsli:

How to Build a 21st Century Financial Practice
FastTrack Coaching
101 Serious Money Selling Tips
101 Tips for Coaching Financial Advisors
101 Tips for Becoming a Preferred Wholesaler
The Intangibles Process
Winning the Inner Game of Selling
Mind Power For Students

Total Achievement Publishing
1005 Battleground Ave.
Greensboro, NC 27408

Cover design by Kerri Lindley
Book design and layout by Dale Smith
Printed in the United States of America

ISBN: 0-9656765-5-2

Testimonials

For *Mastering High Net Worth Selling: The Critical Path*

The financial advisor's reluctance to contact High Net Worth investors is a psychological issue. Matt Oechsli does a superb job of specifically identifying the root cause and prescribing a focused approach to overcoming the problem. A must read for anyone targeting the HNW market – the ultimate book of invisible selling.

Steve Binder
Regional President
Wachovia Securities

This book is a valuable resource for financial advisors who are striving for excellence. You have clearly identified the Achilles heel that can keep us from reaching our full potential as investment professionals. Our team will be using these ideas to continue the growth of our 21st Century Financial Practice.

David J. Bromelkamp, CIMA, CIMC
Senior Vice President – Financial Consultant
RBC Dain Rauscher Senior Consulting Group

A must read for anyone serious about working with high net worth clients. Everyone is talking about wealth management, but no one is telling us how to sell – until now.

F. Lee Bryan III
Managing Director
DB Alex. Brown

Matt's new book is a great follow-up to How to Build a 21st Century Financial Practice. That book guides you on setting up a practice that high net worth investors will covet. His new book teaches you how to fill your practice with the clients you desire.

Jim Burke
Wealth Management Specialist
Sage Rutty and Company

This guidebook for the serious advisor (novice or experienced) is "vintage" Matt Oechsli. Each chapter is designed to help the advisor think about his or her business, evalute what to improve, and then focus on doing it. Matt is combination coach, psychologist, researcher, salesman, and teacher.

Nerine C. Day
Vice President
Merrill Lynch

I think the book is great. Knowing what to do and how to do it is great, but taking action is the absolute key. It's an unbelievable source of information that allows me to fully understand the high net worth selling process.

Jeff Fong
Senior Vice President, Investments
Salomon Smith Barney

Finally, a book that addresses sales skills as they relate to the high net worth. Complete with tactics, fixed daily activities, and scripts, Matt Oechsli ties everything together using the critical path concept – which I think is brilliant. This book is a must read!

Charley Grose
President
RBC Dain Rauscher

This book covers the bases and unravels the "mystery" of high net worth selling. The master coach addresses our deepest fears. Matt takes us by the hand and – step by step – keeps us on course, even allowing us to self correct along the way to a different, infinitely better and once seemingly unattainable business. He converts the dream into a reality. Well done!

Tom Owens
Executive Vice President
Prudential Securities

Oechsli does it again! After revolutionizing the wealth management process with 'How to Build a 21st Century Financial Practice,' Matt takes our profession to even higher levels with his latest work. The underlying 'Critical Path' just may be the secret to the optimal HNW relationship. This is a must read for those who want to be considered in the top one percent of our industry.

Steven M. Samuels
First Vice President, Branch Manager
Prudential Securities

Nothing is more important for registered reps than mastering high net worth selling skills. Once again, Matt is on target and has provided a timely, practical, user-friendly guide.

Rich Santos
Group Publisher
Registered Rep.
Trusts and Estates

Advisors ask: How do I grow my business, break above a specific production level or upgrade my book to HNW clients? Oechsli tells us. Very engaging, well-written and thorough. A must read for every Advisor.

Richard W. Smalley, CFM
Vice President
Wealth Management Advisor
Merrill Lynch

You have condensed into the first three chapters of your book what I have tried to accomplish and teach for over 25 years in the brokerage business. Well done!

Steven Stahlberg
Managing Director
Wachovia Securities

Don't read this book if you're not interested in becoming more successful than you are now! The down-to-earth, hands-on, how-to nature of it will pull you into a winning path. This book delivers a sophisticated mix of psychological principles and proven business strategies.

Mike ter Maat, PhD
Program Development Director
American Bankers Assoc.
Foreword Financial Sales Management Conference

This book lays out a clear step-by-step plan for attracting, selling, and retaining the clients most financial advisors only dream of acquiring. Great job.

Gary C. Valenti, CFP
National Sales Trainer, Annuity Sales
MassMutual Financial Services

Easy to read and track, with specific action steps to follow. You do a nice job of bringing in research and stories to support your theme. For the advisor looking to improve success, why not use a system of proven success.

Mark Warren
Western Senior Vice President
MFS Fund Distributors

Oechsli is an expert on today's high net worth client. He has put together a concise guide which is filled with unique insights and practical advice on how to gain access, build rapport and trailblaze the 'critical path' to success in this complex and growing market.

Ted Williamson
VP, Director of Sales Training
American Skandia

Table of Contents

Preface

It became very clear to me as we evaluated our original research on affluent expectations back in late 1999 and early 2000, that high net worth investors did not want sales people advising them on their finances. Now, over three years later, I'm suggesting that you must *master* high net worth selling skills.

On the surface, I seem to be speaking out of both sides of my mouth, but that's okay. Why? Because what I'm talking about is sales at such a high level that your selling skills are so well honed and practiced, they become seamless, virtually invisible, to your high net worth prospects.

This book began to take shape as it became clear that high net worth selling needed immediate and serious attention. A defining moment occurred in May 2003, when we conducted research to uncover what separates high performance wealth management teams from all the others. We discovered a good number of key differentiating factors, but high net worth selling was not one of them. Less than 28% of the respondents reported high team performance when prospecting for new high net worth clients; 12% even admitted their team's performance was low.

With few exceptions, the entire retail side of the financial services industry is targeting the high net worth segment of the market. That is why teams have emerged so significantly. However, high net worth prospecting and selling is not what teams do. It's what senior financial advisor team members should do, but many are not doing it. Because of that, too many teams are drawn into make-work, waiting for someone to get busy with the challenging task of bringing in new HIGH NET WORTH assets. According to our research, over 70% have failed to do that. Building a 21st century financial practice is of little value without a pipeline continuously being filled with high net worth prospects. High net worth selling, not team building, is the critical path to 21st century success.

We have uncovered several reasons why this is not happening, and have addressed them all in this book. The lack of selling skills is only one of them, and it may not be the most important. Getting face-to-face with

HIGH NET WORTH prospects is. How to do that seamlessly and effectively is the focus of Chapters 5 through 10. But before that can happen, many senior financial advisors must overcome their tendency to be intimidated by people of wealth and power. We have addressed this issue in Chapter 2. Making the transition from investment picker to becoming a go-to high net worth financial quarterback requires a mental and behavioral paradigm shift that many do not fully understand. You will after reading Chapter 3.

With a go-to financial quarterback in the high net worth selling driver's seat, the real reason for having a wealth management team will finally emerge from the shadows and find its proper place in servicing and retaining high net worth clients; clients who have been dissatisfied with their previous financial advisory relationships. Anyone who suggests you don't have to sell to acquire new high net worth clients is either playing with semantics or doesn't know what he or she is talking about.

It's all about assets – getting, managing, retaining, and growing high net worth assets. Guess where it starts!

Matt Oechsli

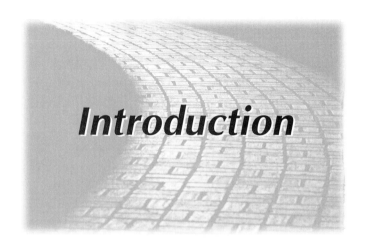

Introduction

Chapter 1

Mastering High Net Worth Selling

1
Mastering HNW Selling

The 21st century financial advisors who will earn the most money, provide the best lifestyles for their families, and enjoy the highest levels of career satisfaction are going to be an elite corps who will excel in doing three things very well:

1. *Get face-to-face* with High Net Worth (HNW) prospects.

2. *Sell* prospects on establishing a long-term financial advisory relationship.

3. *Manage* the financial advisory relationship toward building the level of client loyalty required to turn the relationship into an ongoing referral generator.

Make no mistake about it …

Mastering HNW Selling is your *Critical Path* to building a successful 21st Century Financial Practice.

The concept of *Critical Path* has an interesting origin, dating back to the 1950s when the United States was experiencing strong economic growth. Construction was booming, and one major challenge was to complete building projects in a timely and cost efficient manner, so that the high demand for products and services could be met.

In 1957, M.R. Walker of DuPont and J.E. Kelly of Remington Rand developed a project planning and management technique that provided much-needed answers to three critical scheduling questions:

- How can we accurately estimate how long a complex project will take?

- How can we know, at any time, that we are doing the right activities?

- How can we monitor our progress and reduce the risk of getting off track?

Walker and Kelly answered those questions by developing a way to **define the Critical Path of activities that run through a project and influence everything else that must be accomplished**. The technique became known as the *Critical Path Method* (CPM).

HNW Selling is your Critical Path method. It is characterized by four important factors that have a direct bearing on building a successful 21st Century Financial Practice – and being able to do it within a 12 month time period! This Critical Path method works because ...

1. It focuses on critical activities that must be done each day; activities so vital to your success, that failure to do them will significantly delay your progress. Your Critical Path activities must bring you face-to-face with HNW prospects and enable you to sell them on establishing a long-term financial advisory relationship. Many of the financial advisors we encounter get "stuck" because they are doing the wrong activities.

2. It makes vividly clear which skills you need in order to master the *HNW Selling Process*. Critical Path skills focus on getting face-to-face, building rapport and then clinching and managing the financial advisory relationship. The result is a pipeline continually filled with HNW introductions and referrals.

3. It serves as an activity filter. When you look closely at what it takes to build a 21st Century Financial Practice, you can easily identify 25 to 30 different activities that might need your attention. The Critical Path enables you to set many of those activities aside and focus only on the ones that are critical right now. Because you are continually doing what is really important, you will find that you are gaining the experience and confidence to do all those other activities at precisely the right time.

4. It serves as an activity accelerator. You will monitor your Critical Path activity on a weekly basis, enabling you to make timely adjustments. The weekly cycle of *plan-do-evaluate-adjust* will keep you on track.

This book will teach you how to increase your earnings by mastering the intricacies of the *HNW Selling Process*; a selling process that will reveal unique challenges not mentioned in any other books on sales that we have seen. These challenges are addressed here in detail because they are vital to your HNW Selling success.

The term *High Net Worth (HNW)* will be used throughout this book to label a specific group of affluent investors. The categories of people with serious money to invest are described in the following chart. To simplify and accelerate your reading, we will use *High Net Worth,* and most often *HNW*, to represent that entire range of investors.

- **Affluent, and Emerging Affluent** – those with $100,000 to $1 million in investable assets.
- **HNW** – those with $1 million to $5 million in investable assets.
- **Penta-Millionaires** – those with $5 million to $10 million in investable assets.
- **Ultra HNW** – those with $10 million plus in investable assets.

Source: HNWAdvisor.com

Everyone's Doing It!

I'm sure you have noticed that practically everyone in the financial services industry is targeting HNW investors with hopes of becoming their primary "go-to" financial advisor. That "everyone" includes investment brokers, insurance agents, financial planners, accountants, traditional banks, and even prestigious banks who in the past wouldn't accept an initial investment of less than 5 to 10 million dollars. In between are firms such as Schwab, Vanguard, and even giant pension-fund manager TIAA-CREF who are finding creative ways to penetrate this lucrative segment of the financial services market. By offering new programs with lower fees, personal money managers, and teams of specialists to help with everything from taxes to estate planning, these firms are coming up with new ways to target the entire spectrum of HNW investors.

There are good reasons to be making this effort. According to the San Francisco consulting firm Spectrem Group, there are currently about 2.9 million U.S. households with a net worth of $1 million or more. That is double the 1990 figure. In addition, there are about 14.5 million house-holds with a net worth of $500,000 to $1 million. That is a very substan-tial market segment that is continuing to grow. According to the Merrill Lynch/Cap Gemini Ernst & Young World Wealth Report of 2002, HNW wealth will average 8% annual growth over the next 5 years, reaching $38.5 trillion by the end of 2006. These numbers don't even include the estimated $41 trillion that will be transferred between generations over the next 50 years (HNWAdvisor.com).

We often refer to these substantial, growing HNW segments as low-hang-ing fruit waiting to be picked. It's not simply the numbers. The real opportunity lies in the fact that so many HNW investors are expressing dissatisfaction with their current financial advisor. We initially discov-ered a significant gap between investor expectations and financial advi-sor performance in our 1999 research. This was further confirmed in a 2002 NFO WorldGroup survey where 21% of HNW investors stated they would be better off without a financial advisor. One would expect that all the effort to target this group would now begin to show positive results. Not so. In research done for Quicken in early 2003, 70% of HNW investors said that their faith in financial experts had declined over the past year. Only 30% said they would continue consulting with their stockbroker. Believe it or not, this is truly *good news* for you. Dissatisfaction is the breeding ground of opportunity!

I'd Love To Do It, But...

People of affluence are cautious consumers. As their wealth becomes public, more and more people try to sell them something, and they are quickly turned off by marketing techniques and sales pitches. When any type of broad, impersonal marketing approach is used, they typically resist both the approach and the person using it. This resistance is a more emotional than rational response. Recent scandals on Wall Street involv-ing research analysts have made a skeptical HNW populace even more wary. Facts and data have very little influence at this point if investors don't feel they can trust what is being presented to them – and even less influence if they have trouble understanding the data because it's stated in obscure financial jargon.

HNW investors are looking for a competent financial advisor, backed by a team of experts, who can help them with their wide range of financial protection, investment, disbursement, and philanthropic needs. Many prefer one "go-to" source to coordinate everything from budgeting to estate planning, as well as a half dozen other services. But they will not accept the advice and guidance of someone they cannot trust. Trust and value are the pivotal factors. HNW investors need to trust your competence and your integrity, and they must see true value in what you offer. Initiating a long-term go-to financial advisor relationship is a combined emotional and rational decision based on the experience they have had with you. Our focus in this book is to help you skillfully orchestrate that experience.

Although everyone is "targeting" HNW investors, many are not confident about taking the steps to meet with those investors face-to-face. It seems to be an "I'd love to do it but…" proposition where the "but…" is not always so clear. I sense this hesitation frequently during coaching situations.

Following are the ten areas relating to HNW Selling that I am asked about frequently when coaching veteran financial professionals. Take a few moments to read through the 10 statements below and and record your own thoughts as instructed.

For each of the STATEMENTS below, there are *two sets of questions* for you to answer. Circle YES or NO for each set:

- Do you know WHAT to do and HOW to do it?
- Are you DOING it?

	Know how		Doing it	
1. Find HNW prospects.	Yes	No	Yes	No
2. Effectively contact HNW prospects.	Yes	No	Yes	No
3. Build rapport in a face-to-face meeting with a HNW prospect.	Yes	No	Yes	No
4. Uncover areas of transition and dissatisfaction during a conversation with a HNW prospect.	Yes	No	Yes	No

	Know how		Doing it	
	Yes	No	Yes	No
5. Convince a HNW prospect of the value you bring to the table.	Yes	No	Yes	No
6. Get a HNW prospect to trust you with managing their considerable assets.	Yes	No	Yes	No
7. Convince a HNW prospect to work with you on a fee basis.	Yes	No	Yes	No
8. Overcome objections and reluctance of a HNW prospect to work with you.	Yes	No	Yes	No
9. Close the sale and clinch a long-term financial advisory relationship with a HNW prospect.	Yes	No	Yes	No
10. Get solicited and unsolicited referrals and introductions from HNW clients.	Yes	No	Yes	No

Both response categories are important, but it's the *Doing it* that matters most. You may know what to do and even how to do it, but if you are not doing it, you will not retain confidence in your knowledge and skills for very long. Our goal is to enable you to answer YES to both categories for each question, and do so confidently.

Understanding why even the most experienced financial professionals are often reluctant to take these steps is the first issue we address in this book. Learning well defined and carefully crafted HNW Selling skills and how to use them to find, connect with, and close HNW prospects is the other focus.

You have heard from me, as well as others, that HNW prospects do not want a sales person advising them; yet now we are suggesting that you need to learn well defined and carefully crafted selling skills. To understand this dichotomy, the focus needs to be on "well defined and carefully crafted." HNW prospects do need to be *sold*, so your *selling skills* must be so fine-tuned and well crafted, that they become seamless. *The*

HNW Selling Process we are about to unfold will explain what you need to do. The remainder of the book will teach you how.

The Biggest Motivator in Buying

Now that the market has tumbled, dissatisfaction and skepticism are at an all-time high. What will it take to win HNW investors away from their current financial professionals? It depends on what their biggest motivator for "buying" financial advisory services happens to be. But you can be assured of one thing, they won't decide strictly on the basis of information, data, and facts. It will be first and foremost an emotional response. When they feel comfortable with you and believe they can trust you, they will decide in your favor. They will consider making the buying decision based on feelings, and then they will rationalize that decision based on how much they value your expertise and the way you do business.

Some neuropsychologists now believe that the emotional and rational parts of the brain may be more closely intertwined than previously thought. A study reported in November 2001 by Dr. Dean Shibata of the University of Washington clearly demonstrates that people use the emotional parts of their brain to make personal decisions, even though the task itself may not seem emotional in nature. Further evidence comes from neurologist Antonio Damasio, who found that when someone suffers an injury to the brain section that governs emotion, they will often have trouble making even routine, rational decisions for themselves – even though they may retain normal memory and be capable of solving abstract problems.

This intertwining of the emotional and rational parts of the brain is especially important when prospecting for HNW clients. Before accepting your offer to become their "go-to" financial advisor, they will need to be convinced that you are capable of providing exactly the right financial advice at precisely the right time. Although there is a strong rational component to that decision, before they can come to that conclusion, they must be sold on you. That decision will be largely emotional. **The buying process when serious money is involved begins at the emotional level, evolves to an emotional conclusion, and along the way becomes intertwined with the rational dimension of the decision**. To become seamless, your selling approach must become interlocked with their buying process.

11

Some of the rational dimension actually occurs after the sale is made and you begin working with your new HNW client. As with any intangible service, there can be no test drive before the sale is closed. Consequently, HNW clients will continually evaluate the ongoing experience they have with you, both emotionally and rationally, until they finally conclude that their choice was the right one.

During a seminar at Wharton in March 2000, I presented for the first time the three areas of greatest dissatisfaction that HNW investors have with their financial advisors, based on research we completed in late 1999. Keep in mind that these findings were compiled, presented, and published before some 8 to 9 trillion dollars worth of shareholder value was lost. The three areas of HNW investor dissatisfaction were:

1. Not providing satisfactory value for fees and commissions paid.
2. Not trusting the advisor to give advice that is always in the investor's best interest.
3. Not providing high-quality information for making financial and investment decisions.

Our survey respondents were telling us that they had made an emotional decision to turn assets over to a financial advisor, but their post-decision experience was not measuring up to their expectations. Because their expectations were not supported later by the facts, the seed of dissatisfaction became firmly planted. As we noted earlier, there has not been much improvement since.

Mastering the HNW Selling Process

HNW Selling requires getting face-to-face with a HNW prospect and doing the right things to sell him or her on establishing a business relationship with you as their "go-to" financial quarterback. This is a one-person-at-a-time proposition. To illustrate, let me share an incident that actually occurred as I was writing this chapter.

I received a call from Jay, a successful financial advisor who wanted some advice on personnel matters. As we concluded our discussion, I turned the conversation to HNW Selling. Knowing that Jay had worked hard to master HNW Selling skills, I asked him to tell me how he was progressing.

"Everything is working just like we planned, "Jay responded. "I have 12 to 15 million dollars in the immediate pipeline, and I just received a referral from a new CPA. That now makes five CPAs who are consistently referring business to me. I never would have believed that professional and social networking could produce such results. It's almost too easy!"

As was his nature, Jay was not giving himself enough credit. He had gone far outside his comfort zone to change from being a successful transactional stockbroker to a legitimate financial advisor. Rather than making telephone sales calls all day and keeping score by his daily production numbers, he was now getting out of the office, meeting face-to-face with HNW prospects and centers-of-influence, and consistently tracking his appointments as well as the assets he was attracting to his pipeline.

"Last week I had twelve face-to-face meetings," he answered when I asked about his fixed daily activities. I then asked him to describe the HNW Sales process he was using. He laughed and responded, "Just like you taught me." I was curious to see how he had customized everything, so I pressed him to explain it to me again. What Jay shared with me was beautiful in its simplicity.

"I first take time to develop rapport. Then I explain that I need to profile them and they need to profile us to determine whether there is a match. The reverse psychology of this approach puts them at ease, so I rarely have difficulty getting permission to ask a few general background financial questions. I follow that by explaining the steps of our financial advisory process, including the benefit they will receive from each step. Once the relationship is established, I start collecting the necessary information. It's really quite simple. "

I laughed when he used the word "simple," and reminded him that 14 months earlier this was not the case. Jay was now pursuing his Critical Path, which enabled him to master the fine art of HNW Selling. He hadn't sent out one brochure during the past six months.

HNW Selling becomes seamless with practice, and that is critical. It involves a process of building rapport, connecting with targeted prospects, and clinching the relationship one prospect at a time. But before initiating the process, there are some preparation issues that require your careful attention.

Following is a brief overview of the upcoming chapters and how each will activate and guide you along your Critical Path to HNW Selling success.

Position Yourself to Succeed

- **Overcoming HNW Sales Reluctance** (Chapter 2). HNW Selling is proving to be a significant challenge (the number one challenge) for many financial professionals. One aspect is the *social self-consciousness* problem that many experience when they shift their efforts toward up-market clients. The good news is that it is self-inflicted and can be overcome. We will show you how, and we will help you with other issues related to HNW sales reluctance as well. HNW sales reluctance needs to be put behind you before you step onto the Critical Path and begin your journey.

- **Making the HNW Paradigm Shift** (Chapter 3). To become the go-to financial quarterback that HNW investors seek, an important mental and behavioral paradigm shift is required. The transactional broker, insurance agent, or financial planner who is accustomed to the immediate gratification derived from selling a financial product, must now build long-term relationships, provide an ongoing financial advisory process and learn to live with delayed gratification. To successfully shift gears, these challenges must be mastered internally. This chapter will help you see why the Critical Path concept is vital to successfully making that shift.

- **Finding Qualified HNW Prospects** (Chapter 4). Without an effective HNW prospecting system, your entire HNW Selling process will remain at a standstill. The first step is to determine which HNW niche best fits your background, expertise, and networking possibilities, so you will be in the right position to find and make contact with qualified HNW prospects. I refer to this effort to find HNW prospects as 'skating to the money.'

- **Filling Your Pipeline** (Chapter 5). Arranging an initial face-to-face meeting with a qualified prospect from the HNW investor niche you have targeted will only happen if you keep your prospect pipeline full. As you begin your journey along the Critical Path, you will immediately begin to fill your HNW prospect pipeline. As you establish a high level of professional respect with each HNW client, you will keep that pipeline filled through the introductions and referrals those loyal clients provide.

Get Face-To-Face With HNW Prospects

- **Helping Them KNOW You** (Chapter 6). This goes beyond your name, company, and CFP designation (if you have it). HNW prospects want a glimpse into your personality and character, and that is impossible without face-to-face interaction where opinions can be formed on a visceral level. The way you prospect and how you conduct those early face-to-face interactions, whether by a formal meeting or casual encounter, is where everything begins. Your Critical Path must be paved with face-to-face interactions in order for you to succeed.

- **Helping Them LIKE You** (Chapter 7). People prefer conducting business with people they like. "But what if the chemistry isn't right?" you may be thinking. Deliberately helping people decide they like you is about looking and listening, and then doing the things they appreciate while avoiding the things they do not. It requires adjusting your style to their needs, which enables you to go beyond simply hoping that the chemistry is right.

- **Getting Them To TRUST You** (Chapter 8). When considering a tangible product, the customer can usually try it out before they buy, or at least exchange or even return the product if they are not satisfied. Not so with financial services. They "try out" your services after becoming a client. To become your client, they must first discover specific reasons why they can trust you. When you take the time and effort to establish a know you/like you relationship first, getting them to trust you becomes possible.

Sell HNW Prospects

- **Earning Their RESPECT** (Chapter 9). In your first face-to-face encounters, you will begin to probe into your HNW prospect's financial situation, and that will provide opportunities to display your professional expertise. It is important to ask the right questions and use reverse psychology to communicate that you, as well as they, are using this opportunity to see if there is a proper fit. Describing ways you have helped existing clients will also be valuable. Their body language, facial expressions, and comments will tell you how much they respect what you are telling them.

- **Clinching The Relationship** (Chapter 10).   Building rapport, uncovering commonalties, and constructing an emotional bridge of trust enables you to favorably position yourself with your HNW prospect. *Clinching the relationship* is your ultimate goal, which involves much more than simply closing the sale. It is the culmination of a specific sequence of mini-closes that you will use throughout the *HNW Selling Process*, each enabling you to schedule timely face-to-face interaction and bring closure on key areas at appropriate points. The key is knowing *what* to ask, *when* to ask, and *how* to ask it. The final mini-close comes when your HNW prospect is ready to entrust you with an "I'm ready to do business" decision. At that point, you are well along your Critical Path.

Manage The HNW Client Relationship

- **Delivering What You Promised** (Chapter 11). You conduct business through a series of working meetings that bring you face-to-face with clients on a timely basis. You maintain that momentum as both you and your client carry out defined responsibilities between those meetings. As you earn and build on that client's loyalty, you will receive a very valuable reward for your efforts – introductions and referrals that keep your HNW prospect pipeline full. At this stage, you will be moving down your Critical Path, almost in cruise control. This should be every financial advisor's ultimate goal.

- **Activating Your Critical Path** (Chapter 12). Whatever you presently do every day, whether you believe it's effective or not, you do out of habit. When you reach this point in the book, you will know what you need to do to master the *HNW Selling Process* and follow your Critical Path to success. The only questions left to answer are these: Will you do it? If so, when will you start? We will help you answer those questions and provide you with tools to help you establish your Critical Path and maintain the momentum you need to be successful.

In the world of HNW Selling, it's all about relationships. It's getting up from behind your desk, going out and placing yourself in the path of targeted HNW prospects, building rapport, connecting, and clinching a business relationship with them, one-prospect-at-a-time. It's about following your Critical Path to HNW Selling success. Many are doing it and so can you. This book will help you learn how.

Positioning Yourself to Succeed

2
Overcoming HNW Sales Reluctance

The HNW investor opportunity is like manna from heaven! Financial service firm executives are enthused. Training departments are busy. It's time to get refocused. Everyone's excited, right? Wrong. Become invisible and slip into the offices of the branch managers and financial advisors who are saddled with the task of identifying and finding qualified HNW prospects, with attracting their substantial assets to these new programs and establishing long-term relationships with them. What you will often find is that far too many are sitting in their offices, looking in the rear-view mirror, waiting with blind optimism for the past to reappear, rather than building for a realistic future. They are standing on the sidelines, unaware that the Critical Path described in Chapter 1 even exists. If you are one who lacks the confidence to target HNW investors, you are not alone.

The following comment appeared on a popular financial services discussion forum earlier this year …

> *Just last Friday I played golf with a friend of mine who is worth over $60 million, but I feel like he is untouchable. What would you say to someone in a golf cart who is worth over $60 million?*

If you told this financial advisor exactly what he should say, I suspect you would once again hear, "…but I feel like he is untouchable." The problem here goes beyond not knowing what to say.

What's Really Holding You Back?

Like many financial advisors, this individual says he wants to take his prospecting efforts up-market, but he feels like he is stuck. There is strong evidence that he is wrestling with a very common self-inflicted emotional blockage called *social self-consciousness.*

George Dudley and Shannon Goodson, authors of *The Psychology of Call Reluctance: Earning What You're Worth,* define social self-consciousness

---
21

as "salespeople who shun prospects of wealth, prestige, power, education or social standing." They go on to describe the negative impact on an otherwise healthy sales career that can occur when a salesperson shifts his or her emphasis to up-market clients. Whether the individual or their company initiated the shift does not matter, the impact is the same. The authors also suggest that when this form of call reluctance is detected early, and the proper remedy is provided, it is relatively easy to correct.

If you see yourself in the above example, be assured that this is not a case of low self-esteem, low goal motivation, or a lack of assertiveness. In fact, it often happens with those who are above average in all three – except when they approach prospects of wealth, prestige, and power. Here are some signs that suggest the presence of social self-consciousness.

1. Setting HNW prospecting goals, but failing to follow through.
2. Exaggerating the power, prestige, and fame of HNW individuals, both in your own thinking and verbally to others. The above comment from the discussion forum is a good example.
3. Telling others, "I'm not really interested in that segment of the market."
4. Feeling self-conscious and becoming tongue-tied when in the presence of HNW people.
5. The tendency to try to intimidate people at lower levels in the organization as a way of compensating for your own frustrations with feeling intimidated around wealth.

As Dudley and Goodson helpfully point out, these emotional boundaries are all self-inflicted, which means they can be overcome – with effort. The first step is to make a quick assessment to see if social self-consciousness might be something that is holding you back from taking the first step on your Critical Path.

Evaluating Social Self-Consciousness

As with any effort to look closely at yourself, this evaluation requires both honesty and courage. Otherwise the effort has little value.

Is social self-consciousness a problem with you? There are only two possible answers – *yes* or *no*. So take a deep breath. Then read each statement and circle YES or NO on your right.

Is this a problem?

I have set goals for attracting HNW prospects, but I haven't begun prospecting that group yet.	YES	NO
When pushed, I frequently give some reason why I am not interested in pursuing HNW prospects.	YES	NO
I often feel uneasy in the presence of people I view as having wealth, power, prestige, or fame.	YES	NO
I sometimes catch myself being somewhat tongue-tied when conversing with people of wealth and prestige.	YES	NO
I must admit that I tend to exaggerate the power, prestige, and influence of people with wealth.	YES	NO
There are times when I talk down to and treat people in support positions worse than I should – to make them feel the way I do around people of power and influence.	YES	NO
I need and want to raise the bar so I can target HNW investors, but I really feel stuck.	YES	NO

The key issue is this: How significant is social self-consciousness in blocking you from enthusiastically targeting high net worth clients? To determine the answer, add up the number of times you circled YES.

Write the number here: _____ Circle the NUMBER on the continuum below.

Significant Action is Needed	Moderate Action is Needed	NO Action is Needed
7 6 5	4 3 2	1 0

I cannot emphasize the importance of being completely honest with yourself on this issue. Nobody likes to admit to a weakness, particularly when it involves intimidation. As a result, there is a tendency for some financial professionals to lie to themselves, trying to convince themselves that they have no problem when they are face-to-face with a HNW prospect.

> *I was asked to spend time with a father-daughter team to discuss their business development efforts. The father had developed a healthy asset base. His daughter, armed with an MBA, technology savvy, and good process skills was attempting to transition them from being a one-dimensional group of stockbrokers into a 21st Century Financial Practice. She suggested that their main task was to get the father to be more active developing new business.*

> *"All we need to do is get more activity. Once we get a prospect in our office and take them through our investment process, we close virtually 100%," explained the daughter. Father nodded approvingly. So when I responded, "Then obviously you are not dealing with HNW prospects," the daughter protested. Dad waved her off and said, "If we're honest with ourselves, we are not targeting high enough. We both need to do a better job of getting in front of true HNW prospects and stop making excuses about why we can't seem to find them."*

Because I know how HNW prospects make decisions, I was convinced that this team was not dealing with them. They admitted that I was right. Both were suffering from social self-consciousness, but the daughter kept saying that she had young children and would not trade her family time for spending all that time trying to find and get face-to-face with HNW prospects. This was a curious objection from a mother who was already working close to ten hours every working day. Honesty is essential!

Taking Action To Break Out and Move Ahead

Your next step is to take appropriate action to overcome any aspects of social self-consciousness that are holding you back. Following are several suggestions.

1. Preparation

   • Develop your list of ideal HNW prospects. Begin with people linked to your 25 top clients, then go to your centers-of-influence, and finally explore the local media for money in motion and promotions. Use the strategies and methods that will be described in Chapter 4.

   • Determine your "value hook". Whether you are confident you can save HNW clients money on their taxes, re-allocate their portfolio, or review their Mutual Fund and annuity statements, the secret is to link a specific area of expertise to an area where you can add value. Use the strategies and techniques covered in Chapters 5 and 6.

2. Mental Rehearsal

   Immediately before each face-to-face encounter, visualize the exact results you want. Whether you will be on the golf course, at a committee meeting, or bumping into a HNW prospect through a carefully orchestrated "coincidental" meeting at your local Starbucks – if you can visualize a successful encounter in your mind, the image you create will have a positive impact on your results. Top athletes and actors have used mental rehearsal for years.

3. Action

   Regardless of your preparation and visualization, your apprehension will not totally disappear. The key is to not allow those feelings to keep you from doing what you need to do. Following are three techniques that will help you to relax, beat away the emotional demons attempting to sabotage your efforts, and give you a better chance at performing well:

   • *Mental Signal* – I have seen good results when I have clients visualize a candle flame whenever they sense doubt or feel nervous. Simply visualize a candle flame in your mind, take a deep breath, exhale slowly, and feel the anxiety flush out of your system as you exhale. When you are finished, mentally blow out the candle flame.

- *Rubber Band* – Place a rubber band around your wrist. When you catch a negative thought or feeling entering your mind, stop it by snapping the rubber band (back of your hand, not underneath). Those negative thoughts will stop immediately.

- *Positive Affirmations* – Whenever you catch yourself having a negative thought, replace it with a positive affirmation. For example, if you're thinking, "I'm too nervous..." — replace it with, "I'm relaxed and confident." This works especially well right after you blow out the candle flame or snap the rubber band.

These techniques work because they serve to realign your thinking. Most, if not all, negative feelings and anxiety are caused by the view we take of situations, not the situations themselves. If we keep thinking about all the bad things that might happen, our body accepts those thoughts as truth because it cannot distinguish fact from fiction.

Your Conscious Thought Management ACTION PLAN

Becoming aware that you have a social self-consciousness problem and initiating the actions above may be all you need to get unstuck and overcome any HNW reluctance you may be experiencing. If so, that's great! However, there will be new challenges to face as you will discover the steps you must take to successfully attract, service, and retain HNW clients.

Using *Conscious Thought Management* to program your mind for success can be critically important. Everything you are today is the result of your collective thinking up to this point. Everything you will become will also be influenced by your thoughts from this point forward. If you want to experience growth and increase your probability of success, create a mental picture of what you want to become, and then concentrate on that mental picture until it becomes reality.

The following four techniques will help you create an effective *Conscious Thought Management Action Plan*. The first three are very easy to implement and can (should) be done each day. The fourth will take more preparation, but is easily implemented as well.

Technique #1: Start Out Right

During the first hour after awakening, the subconscious mind is more amenable to new programming than at any other time. As soon as you arise in the morning say, "I feel terrific! I feel great!" Then spend 20 to 30 minutes reading or listening to something inspirational, motivational, or instructional. Do not listen to the news or anything that might stimulate negative thinking.

Technique #2: Get Back On Track

All people have "down times" during the day. We describe them as coffee breaks, meal breaks, or traveling between calls. Those are the times we are most susceptible to negative self-talk, especially if we have just had a bad experience or are struggling with social self-consciousness. From now on, make certain you fill your "down times" by listening to inspirational messages or reading that will fill your conscious mind with positive thoughts.

Technique #3: Associate With the Right People

People we associate with often have the greatest influence on us. If you are serious about becoming a go-to financial quarterback for HNW clients, it is important to associate with people who will positively reinforce your thoughts and efforts. This may mean avoiding someone with whom you now associate and/or adding someone new to your reference group. Make your associations a choice – and choose carefully!

Technique #4: Create a Self-Affirmation CD or Tape

Garbage in, garbage out. The best way to take heed of this warning is to replace "garbage" in with a habit of daily self-affirmation. It requires an initial effort to write and record a CD or tape that you can play over and over, but you will be delighted with the results. Creating a self-affirmation CD or tape is actually quite simple. It is based on the 7-7-7 rule:

- 7 affirmation statements,
- Repeated 7 times each, and
- Spaced 7 seconds apart.

It is most beneficial to look at your total life and seek balance when creating your 7 affirmation statements. Focus on areas that you WANT TO CHANGE and areas that you DON'T WANT TO NEGLECT.

To achieve balance, I suggest that you develop your affirmation statements as follows …

- 3 or 4 statements focused on areas relating to HNW prospecting.
- 3 or 4 statements focused on any combination of the following: physical health, mental health, spiritual, marriage, family, social, educational, personal growth.

The words you select for your affirmation statements are very important. They will determine the pictures that are formed in your subconscious mind. Following are some guidelines.

1. PERSONAL – Begin each statement with such words as …
   I am… I have… It's easy for me to… I enjoy… I love…

   Do not say: *My manager will praise me if I meet face-to-face with more HNW prospects.*

   Say: *I enjoy meeting face-to-face with HNW prospects.*

2. POSITIVE – Focus on what you ideally want in the future. Leave your problems behind.

   Do not say: *I am no longer worrying about my physical health.*

   Say: *I am healthy and fit.*

3. PRESENT TENSE – Say it as if it is true right now. This will prompt your subconscious mind to act automatically as if what you are saying IS reality.

   Do not say: *I will become knowledgeable about the wealthy small business owners in our area.*

   Say: *I am knowledgeable about the wealthy small business owners in our area.*

4. COMPARISON FREE – Comparing yourself to others creates a false sense of reality in your mind. Commit to acquiring the qualities of the high achievers you admire, but do not compare yourself with them.

Do not say: *I am going to improve my elevator speech to be better than Bill.*

Say: *It is easy for me to articulate my value to HNW prospects and centers-of-influence.*

5. PRIVATE – Affirmations are for private use. Don't share them with anyone except a working partner who is using the same technique. People not involved in *Conscious Thought Management* tend not to understand. Some may even try to sabotage your efforts, even though they believe they are trying to help you. By keeping your affirmation statements to yourself, you will be able to say what you really want to say.

Here are three steps you can use to write each of your seven Affirmation Statements.

1. Think of a dimension of your life that you want to change. Write that CHANGE AREA on a piece of paper.

2. Imagine yourself in a situation where you have already made that change and are enjoying the results. Describe that IMAGE.

3. Use what you imagined to guide you in writing a powerful AFFIRMATION STATEMENT (as shown on next page).

Notes: _____

_____

_____

_____

_____

Example:

> **Change Area:** I would like to be confident with HNW prospecting.
>
> **Image:** I am introduced to a HNW prospect by a HNW client. I am full of confidence and positive energy, and I make natural eye contact when shaking hands. My use of reverse psychology in suggesting that we both need to discover if there is a fit causes the prospect to compliment my professionalism.
>
> **Affirmation Statement:** I am confident and able to bring high energy to each encounter with HNW prospects.

Following are some samples of HNW affirmation statements that Financial Advisors have successfully used to overcome their HNW sales reluctance:

- I command professional respect effortlessly when I am with HNW prospects.
- I eagerly and confidently look forward to meeting with HNW prospects.
- I handle the financial affairs of a select group of HNW families.
- I consistently provide high quality, valued service to my HNW clients.
- I know how to gain the trust of HNW prospects.
- I am a HNW prospecting machine.
- I prospect every day for new HNW clients.
- Everywhere I go and in everything I do, I look for HNW prospecting opportunities.
- My HNW Selling skills are seamless.
- I am always under control when in the presence of HNW prospects.
- I build rapport with HNW prospects quickly.
- I ask for HNW introductions and referrals at every opportunity.
- I am totally focused on activities that enhance my HNW prospecting efforts.

An effective method for developing and using affirmation statements effectively is to place each one on a 3 x 5 card. Carry the cards with you everywhere you go. You can then refer to them whenever you feel the need, knowing the kind of extra energy that reviewing your affirmation statements can provide.

Conscious thought management is only half of the solution. The other half is *action*. If you are saying *"I enjoy meeting with HNW prospects"* seven times each day, then you are talking the right walk. However, you also need to walk the talk so that your action reflects your affirmation. Your Critical Path will not exist unless and until you take action, which is why this book has ten more chapters.

3

Making the HNW Paradigm Shift

We recently received a call from a financial advisor who has been in the business about three years. Having been a psychologist in his former life, he was especially enjoying the people interaction side of the business. My goodness, he even liked cold calling. We were having an enjoyable conversation, and I was waiting for him to begin asking about how he could attract more HNW clients. But that is not what happened.

He told me that he had been exploring our web site, and that he had purchased and read *How to Build a 21st Century Financial Practice*. "I really enjoyed reading the book," he said. "It helped me a lot. In fact, I have decided that's not the route I want to go." He then went on to explain that he had decided to build his business to service lower net worth clients. Despite the pressure from his firm to shoot higher, he believed that people with $50 to $150 thousand to invest needed and deserved sound investment advice and were being overlooked, and that's where he wanted to focus his efforts. He realized that he would end up with more clients that way, but he was prepared to provide the support system to serve them well. His Critical Path will take on a more traditional shape and head in a different direction.

Your First HNW Sale

If your goal is to target HNW investors, does that story make you wonder if you are making the right decision? Are you clear about your motives? Is it really worth the effort? Could this psychologist turned financial advisor simply be struggling with the social self-consciousness problem we talked about in Chapter 2? I ask these questions because it's important to recognize that your first HNW sale must be to yourself. Without a doubt, this is your most important sale. Spending 12 months transforming your financial practice is no simple task, and yet you must be committed to doing exactly that, one step at a time. If you are not sold on what you're trying to achieve, your steps will become heavy, you will stray off your Critical Path, and the experience will grind you down until your journey comes to a hault.

In our earlier book, *How To Build a 21st Century Financial Practice,* we outlined a series of steps that enable you to build or transform your financial practice with the specific goal of targeting HNW clients. That book clearly defines what we would call the *outer game* of transforming your practice. This book focuses on the *inner game* that you must master to successfully achieve that goal.

Psychologists tell us that how sold we are on accomplishing something depends on *our motivation strength.* Based on research by David C. McClelland of Harvard and John W. Atkinson of The University of Michigan, it seems that our motivation strength is at its peak when we believe there is about a 50% probability that we can achieve our goals. This means we will not become self-motivated toward pursuing a goal when the probability of goal success is either *virtually certain* (100% probability) or *virtually impossible* to attain (0% probability). Nor will we become self-motivated by unrealistic expectations imposed by others. In fact, failure by financial advisors to meet unrealistically high managerial expectations typically leads to high rates of attrition, both voluntary and involuntary.

The McClelland and Atkinson research suggests that the greatest level of motivation to transform your business will occur when you believe that you have about a 50/50 chance of successfully attracting, servicing, and earning the loyalty of a specific number of HNW clients within a specific time frame. Let's assume, for example, that you have committed to bringing in 15 new HNW clients over the next 12 months. That will require mastering the *HNW Selling Process* and doing some serious HNW sales activity every working day. If you believe you have a 50/50 chance of achieving that 15 new HNW clients goal, you will be maximizing your motivational juices. That confidence will *pull* you forward. Any anxiety you feel will *push* you ahead. Together, that push and pull combination will provide you with the determination to win the inner game and succeed.

Maximizing Your Achievement Drive

I'd like you to take out a piece of paper and at the top write the heading: **Today's REALITY**. Under that heading, write down exactly where you are right now, using the following seven items.

1. Your current client base – the number of clients and households, and the assets you manage for them.

2. Your current client profile – the number of clients who fit into the HNW category. I suggest using a minimum of $250,000 in investable assets. Divide your remaining clients into two other categories: 1) Those who can be upgraded to HNW status within the next 5 years, and 2) Others.

3. How many of your HNW clients currently look to you as their *Go-To Financial Quarterback?*

4. The specific financial services you now provide to those HNW clients – both investment advice services and planning-based services such as financial planning, private banking, tax advice, insurance, education planning, retirement planning, and estate planning.

5. Your current minimum investable asset requirement for accepting new clients.

6. The specific methods you use to attract new clients.

7. Anything else about your current practice that you believe is relevant.

Place a second piece of paper right next to the first one. At the top, write the heading: **Tomorrow's DREAM**. First, write a Target Date for achieving your dream of transforming your business into a 21st Century Financial Practice targeting HNW clients. Focus on 12 months from now.

Once you have selected that date, across from each item write down how each of the 7 items will have changed by that date ...

1. How many clients and households will you have, and what will the total assets you manage for them be?

2. How many of those clients will be in your HNW category? Will you have raised the minimum asset level to $250,000 — $1 million – higher? How many clients will there be in your Upgrade to HNW category; in your Other Clients category?

3. How many of those HNW clients will you be serving as their *Go-To Financial Quarterback?*

4. What specific financial solutions, investment instruments, and planning based services will you (with the help of your financial advisory team) be offering to HNW clients?

5. When prospecting for new clients, what will be your minimum investable asset requirement?

6. What specific methods will you be using at that point to attract new clients? They will all be HNW clients, right?

7. What else will characterize your practice that is a change from what you are doing now?

When you have completed the above, look carefully at each list and ask yourself the following three questions:

Q1: How wide is the GAP between Today's REALITY and Tomorrow's DREAM as I have defined it?

Q2: Will bridging this GAP require simply doing more of what I do now, but doing it better — or will it require a significant shift away from what I do now, using new strategies and techniques, and learning a new set of skills?

Q3: Do I believe today that I have at least a 50/50 change of successfully bridging that GAP?

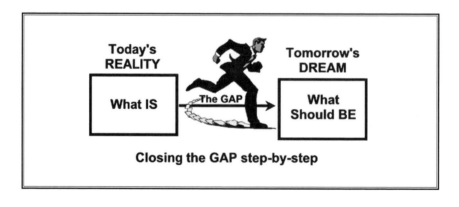

Closing the GAP step-by-step

When you look at the gap that exists between where you are now and where you want to go, you need to be confident that you can close that gap. Because of that, your answer to the second question is most critical. If you have already successfully positioned yourself as a *go-to financial quarterback* for HNW clients, the transition will be a "doing more of what I do now, but constantly finding ways to do it better" situation. If that is not the case, you may be able to identify more closely with Tim.

A highly successful stockbroker, at his peak Tim had raised his production to over the two million dollar mark. A 20 year veteran, Tim enjoyed the good life: multiple luxury cars, boats, and dual residency. He had developed his business cold-calling, worked hard, rode the bull market, and never left his office during the working day. When the market closed, Tim was gone. His business was completed for that day. That was then. At the time of this writing, Tim's business is down over 35 percent, and Tim is feeling pain. Intellectually he understands the importance of moving up-market and making some changes.

"Where do I find all these wealthy people?" he asked me in the hall following a speech I had given, continuing in a whining voice before allowing me to respond, "Nobody is telling me where to find these High Net Worth prospects. I come from a working class background and have never traveled in wealthy circles."

Pursuing HNW prospects was something that had never entered Tim's mind, and making the transition to become a go-to HNW financial quarterback was proving to be a major hurdle.

As we discussed the matter, Tim insisted that he was no longer simply a stockbroker; he was a financial advisor. He said he had become very skilled at picking stocks (in a bull market), but he also sold mutual funds, and he would offer annuities whenever sensing an opportunity. I pointed out that a financial advisor who uses more than one investment platform can still be functioning in the old paradigm. It's only when you synthesize these investment specialties with all the other aspects of wealth management and can provide an integrated financial advisory process that you bridge the gap and become a go-to HNW financial quarterback. In addition, you must know how to find and attract HNW prospects.

Like so many financial professionals today, Tim had decided to target HNW investors. He assumed the new title of *Wealth Advisor*, a title that his firm had provided. But, he neglected to take a careful look at what making that transition required. He simply was not ready to shift gears and enter the new paradigm. He was not ready because he had not yet made his most important sale, and he was in denial about having any type of HNW call reluctance slowing him down. Tim was still searching for his Critical Path.

Getting Ready to Shift Gears

When you create your Today's REALITY list and match it with your Tomorrow's DREAM list, you can envision the gap between them, but you may not fully understand what will be required to close that gap. Without understanding those requirements, it's difficult to calculate whether or not you are maximizing your achievement drive. We will spend the rest of this chapter clarifying those requirements – and helping you develop that 50/50 level of confidence.

The first thing to understand is that as a *go-to HNW financial quarterback* of the 21st Century, you must do these eight tasks very well.

1. Master the HNW Selling Process, and take the lead in prospecting for new HNW clients who match your Ideal Client Profile.

2. Maintain a high level of interaction with each HNW client.

3. Possess a wide breadth and depth of knowledge about the wealth management products and services offered in eight key areas.

- Budgeting, cash flow management, banking, and emergency planning

- Insurance applications for wealth transfer, tax management, wealth preservation, inheritance planning, wealth accumulation, and risk management

- Investments and portfolio management

- Education planning

- Life-event planning

- Tax planning

- Retirement, long-term care, and estate planning

- Charitable giving

4. Be reasonably knowledgeable about each product and service, and be capable of explaining how each integrates with all the others.

5. Be familiar enough with each HNW client's needs to know when to bring in a particular specialist.

6. Form strategic partner relationships with skilled specialists and establish the right type of working agreement and compensation arrangement with each.

7. Build and manage a financial advisory team made up of staff and strategic partners, and keep them focused on serving HNW clients.

8. Keep up with ongoing financial product and service developments and be familiar enough with your HNW client needs to know what to add, and when to make the recommendation.

This book focuses on the first two tasks, and those are precisely what you need to begin your journey down your Critical Path. Our *How to Build a 21st Century Financial Practice* book and *Creating a Successful 21st Century Financial Practice KIT* address the last six.

> By actively pursuing your Critical Path tasks, everything else you need to do will be automatically pulled into play when the time is right. That's the power of the Critical Path concept.

If you have been successful by following a specific pattern of thinking and behavior, it's only natural to assume that same pattern (or paradigm) will continue to make you successful in the future, even when you are thrust into a totally new and different situation. Tim, our "highly successful stockbroker" is a prime example. His biggest problem was his past success.

By "riding" the bull market, working hard and mastering his cold-calling skills, Tim was able to enjoy a high level of stockbroker success. And he earned it! He was on the phone, every day, getting people to buy and sell stocks and mutual funds. Think for a moment about the mental and behavioral habits this type of selling requires.

Successful Transactional Selling Skills

- Perfect your telephone cold calling technique – your most critical skill.

- Avoid face-to-face, interpersonal interaction – it takes too much time.

- Measure results each day (each hour, if you are willing).

- Thrive on instant gratification.

- Check a few client portfolios for buy/sell possibilities.

- Start fresh each day – new people to contact and sell.

Remember what a *21st century go-to HNW financial quarterback* must be able to do? It is definitely not transactions; it's all about process. The *HNW Selling Process* plus your *Financial Advisory Process* enable you to build a unique relationship with each HNW client, and to deliver what you sell. The mental and behavioral transition is significant.

Successful Go-To HNW Financial Quarterback Skills

- Perfect your networking skills in order to generate the needed introductions and referrals – and your telephone technique for arranging an initial face-to-face meeting with qualified HNW prospects.

- Become skilled in and thriving on face-to-face, interpersonal interaction during the selling and the financial advisory processes.

- Measure results incrementally, weekly -> monthly -> quarterly -> yearly.

- Learn to manage and thrive on delayed gratification, both financial and psychological.

- Exercise a leadership role in managing and coordinating each client's financial affairs, including protecting and building each client's portfolio.

- Stay fresh each day – through experiencing the progressive realization of the goals and objectives you have set.

The real issue in shifting gears is entering into a new pattern of thinking and doing; a new paradigm with a new set of rules for achieving success.

These transitions typically happen incrementally. Remember Jay, our success story in Chapter 1? It took him over two years to make the shift.

The *21st Century Go-To HNW Financial Quarterback* PROFILE

The following ten items describe key elements in making the transition. For each element, circle the number that best represents where you are at this time:

> 4 – I have successfully made the transition
> 3 – I am making excellent progress
> 2 – I have started the effort, but I am not very far along
> 1 – I am just beginning the effort
> 0 – I have not yet started making this transition

===

1. Skillfully maintain a high level of interaction with each client.　　　　0 1 2 3 4

2. Be reasonably conversant about each of your wealth management products and service, and how they all interrelate with each other.　　　　0 1 2 3 4

3. Know your products and clients well enough to know when to bring in a specialist.　　　　0 1 2 3 4

4. Form strategic partnerships with specialists, making certain you have the right working arrangement and compensation agreement with them.　　　　0 1 2 3 4

5. Build a Financial Advisory Team of the right staff and strategic partners, and keep everyone focused on meeting client needs.　　　　0 1 2 3 4

6. Keep up with financial product/service developments and client needs well, so that you know what to add and when.　　　　0 1 2 3 4

7. Generate needed introductions and referrals through perfecting networking and phone techniques.　　　　0 1 2 3 4

8. Thrive on face-to-face, interpersonal interaction during 0 1 2 3 4
   both the selling and financial advisory processes.

9. Recognize that a portfolio's return depends more on   0 1 2 3 4
   managing asset allocation than on specific stock, bond,
   or mutual fund picks.

10. Stay fresh each day through the progressive realization 0 1 2 3 4
    of goals and objectives rather than on immediate
    financial and psychological gratification.

===

Following are suggestions that will help you benefit from this assessment.

Draw a line to connect the numbers you circled for each element. That will allow you to see the ten elements as an integrated whole.

- The elements with a 3 or 4 circled indicate your present areas of strength.

- Those with a 0 or 1 circled indicate your present limitations.

Look at the items circled 0, 1, or 2, and consider these points.

- Identifying what is blocking your progress is half the battle. If you have given an honest answer to each question, you now know what you need to overcome.

- Those areas where you circled 2, or even 1, suggest you are already making an effort. By continuing to capitalize on those areas, you can accelerate your overall effort.

- Admit your limitations and ask people you trust to help you.

As you progress through this book, you will define your Critical Path required to make this paradigm shift within the next 12 months, or perhaps even sooner. You will discover new ways to build the momentum you need to push your way through those blockages and become the type of *go-to HNW financial quarterback* you envision.

Paving Your Road to Success

Any road construction expert will tell you that the materials selected to pave a road will determine how long and how well that road will be traveled before potholes and other signs of deterioration appear. Borrowing from a popular book title, your HNW Selling Process must become a *road well traveled*. Conviction, confidence, and competency are the ingredients that will serve you well on your journey.

1. ***Conviction***. This means to believe without proof. When you initiate a long-term relationship with a HNW prospect, that's exactly what you are asking that prospect to do. It is also what you must do. You must be convinced that the goals you established for your business are both *believable* and *achievable*.

   You must be convinced that if you do the hard work, venture outside your comfort zone, perform your fixed daily activities, and maintain your metrics scorecards, you can achieve your goals as they pull you through all the ups and downs of making this important paradigm shift, away from daily transactions to focusing on longer term HNW Selling and financial advisory processes.

   Review your business plan. Ask yourself: Are my goals believable? By performing my fixed daily activities, are those goals achievable? Then, check your confidence.

2. ***Confidence***. This can be either the pillar or killer of success. Confident people don't have to sit around thinking and talking about what they should do. They get up and go do it. Too much thinking draws us into a NEGATIVE Programming Cycle:

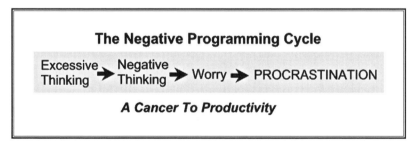

We refer to this malady as "paralysis of perfection." Financial professionals who struggle with social self-consciousness and/or making the paradigm shift to become a *go-to HNW financial quarterback* sometimes think "everything has got to be in place before I get started."

Nothing could be further from the truth. The most effective method for building confidence is *doing* specific activities that are directly linked to a serious goal. You then become ...

• Convinced that your goals are the right ones.

• Confident to take your next step toward your goals.

• Confident that you have the professional expertise to take that next step.

• Confident that taking that next step will not only advance you toward your goals, it will also enable you to gain the additional expertise and added confidence to take the step that comes next.

It is time to set procrastination aside as you replace all that negative programming with the POSITIVE Programming Cycle.

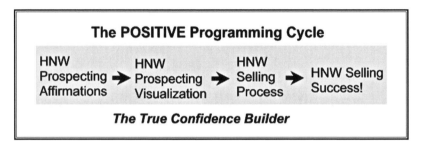

The POSITIVE Programming Cycle

HNW Prospecting Affirmations ➡ HNW Prospecting Visualization ➡ HNW Selling Process ➡ HNW Selling Success!

The True Confidence Builder

Following the Positive Programming Cycle builds confidence. Do it, and you will achieve competency.

3. *Competency*. It evolves from experience done with confidence, not by taking classes or reading books. Knowledge makes you competent when you apply it, make mistakes, adjust, and then do it better. This is especially true for HNW Selling. Without transforming daily activity into filling the pipeline, building rapport, connecting, and clinching the relationship, it is extremely difficult to master the level of selling professionalism required to transform affluent prospects into ideal clients.

Competency is also the product of doing the right things. Certainly services like financial planning, asset allocation, money management, and client-based management are important and must be performed with utmost competency. But you won't have that opportunity without mastering the *HNW Selling Process.* Because the decision to work with you is primarily emotional, the largest incomes will go to those who possess the best selling and relationship management skills, not the best financial planning expertise. So ponder these questions:

- Do you know how to connect in an affluent social setting and then use a financial impact point to open the door, quickly create dissatisfaction, and then position yourself as a HNW financial solutions provider?

- When asked, are you able to explain your work in a succinct and intriguing manner that creates curiosity and a follow-up question?

- Have you developed a *value hook* that is linked to your work but very specific to a HNW prospect? (For example: tax reduction, portfolio re-allocation, or a mutual fund and annuity statement review.)

- Are you skilled at developing rapport and generating trust? Asking questions? Discussing fees?

Once you're convinced you have the right goals and are actively pursuing your Critical Path one confident step at a time, your capabilities will steadily improve. Jay's goals changed from being a million dollar producer to developing a business plan and metrics score card system that focused on building a 21st Century Financial Practice geared to handle every aspect of a HNW client's financial affairs. His efforts to overcome *social self-consciousness* (and he had it) were aided by the pull of his business plan, the push of his metrics scorecard and his willingness to master the necessary skills.

If you apply the principles covered in this chapter, you can activate your *HNW Positive Programming Cycle* and maximize your achievement drive by committing to HNW goals which you believe you have at least a 50/50 chance of achieving. Then you can rest assured that you have a 100% probability of becoming a successful *21st century go-to HNW financial quarterback.* With conviction, confidence and competency, you will no longer need to worry about competition.

4

Finding Qualified HNW Prospects

Without an effective HNW prospecting system, your entire HNW Selling process will remain at a standstill. Your pipeline is the benchmark of how effectively you are staying on your Critical Path. You must keep your pipeline full of qualified prospects who are getting to *know you*, *like you*, and *trust you*. The key is to continually arrange initial face-to-face meetings with qualified prospects from the HNW market niche you have targeted. HNW Selling begins with that initial face-to-face meeting.

The question I am probably asked most is "Where do I find HNW prospects?" which is often followed by "If I could find them, I know I could close them." The thought going through my mind at that moment is, "Yeah — right!" There is a glaring false logic here. Think this through with me.

- If you are asking where to find HNW prospects, that means you have not made a real effort to find them in the past. In fact, you may have actually avoided them – which suggests a possible HNW sales reluctance problem. (see Chapter 2)

- If you avoid spending time with HNW people, you cannot be certain of what they are really like or how to approach them.

- If you are not certain what HNW people are really like, and are hesitant to approach them, you cannot have the slightest notion what it will take to *sell* them.

- Since you don't have the slightest notion what it will take to sell them, you will probably resort to some old "tried 'n true" methods, hoping to net positive results.

Coincidentally, I was asked to review two marketing campaigns targeting HNW investors during the time we were completing the final edit on this book. Both involved seminars, and both groups were using radio campaigns to "invite" their target audience to attend. One client was using her own voice in the ads; the other, a local sports celebrity. In both cases, the ads were professionally produced at a substantial cost.

Do you think these marketing efforts will attract HNW people with at least $250,000 in investable assets? I think you know the answer. Consider carefully the faulty logic that led to these decisions.

Q: How successful have you been in using seminars to attract HNW prospects in the past?
A: Not very. We've brought in a few new clients with between $50,000 and $100,000 in investable assets, but not many.

Q: What are you doing differently this time that you hope will attract prospects with at least $250,000 in investable assets?
A: We are broadcasting on the most popular radio station in the area. We are using a well-known sports celebrity in the ads (and at the seminar in one case). The ad content addresses issues we believe HNW people care about.

Q: What kind of success do you expect?
A: We have no idea. We hope to attract a few HNW prospects, but we'll have to see.

Q: In all honesty, what is the real reason you are using this approach to try and attract HNW prospects?
A: Because we don't know any other way to find them.

If someone with $50,000 to invest shows up, they will know how to help that prospect, and how to close them. They've done it before. If a HNW prospect shows up, will they really know what to do? Actually, that's probably a moot question. There is only a remote chance that a HNW prospect will be attracted by a short, vague radio ad about a public seminar.

Prospecting for HNW clients certainly begins with finding them, and ultimately ends with closing them. But HNW Selling is more than that — much more. If you happen to live in an area where the lakes freeze over in the winter, and you love to go skating on those lakes, you will know what I mean. You don't just find a lake and go skating. The skates you choose, the sharpness of the blades, the condition of the ice, the clothing you wear, and the movements you've learned all work together to make it a pleasurable winter outing (or not!). When you watch a professional skater, you realize how seamless all that has become for them.

As a financial professional, the elements of HNW Selling must also become seamless for you. That's why I call HNW Selling *skating to the money*.

What You Need is a System

Your *HNW Prospecting System* should be characterized by the following:

1. HNW prospecting is a **high priority**. This means no avoidance patterns. You never wait until you're desperate or don't have anything better to do.

2. HNW prospecting is a **planned activity**. At the beginning of each week, you define the number of new HNW face time appointments you must have during that week to keep your pipeline "full." Then you …

   • Schedule adequate time to find qualified HNW prospects.

   • Schedule adequate time to contact those qualified HNW prospects and arrange face time with them.

   • Enter all activities into your *Weekly Metrics Scorecard* and day planner.

3. You use a **variety of methods** to find and contact qualified prospects. Your selection isn't based on what others say should work best, but on what experience shows works best for you. You continually evaluate which methods are giving you the best-qualified HNW prospects with the least amount of time and effort. The emphasis here is on "best qualified."

4. You are actively involved with **prospecting each and every day** – no exceptions! Why? Because prospecting is the heart of your Critical Path.

You are being asked to make a paradigm shift in your scorekeeping. No longer will you be tracking daily production numbers, reminiscent of the old transactional days. You are now going to track the progress of every HNW prospect with whom you've had a face-to-face encounter. It's simple in concept, but a challenge to apply.

> *A wealth management team had just spent 30 minutes describing and explaining their wealth management process and their success. It sounded like they had all of their bases covered. Then a comment was made about "not being able to afford losing another quality client," and I had my opening. I asked about their production. It was down more than 30%, and had been declining for two consecutive years, from a high of 2.2 million. I asked them how many HNW prospects they had in their pipeline. Not only did they not have a pipeline, they were not very pleased about being asked. As the truth came out, they admitted to having lost confidence because of the three-year decline in the market. In the 90's they didn't need to prospect much because unsolicited referrals simply came to them.*

This illustrates why prospecting must be a high priority and a planned activity. Your commitment to keep your pipeline full is where your Critical Path begins. As you discover what this requires, your ultimate prospecting goal will be to arrange face time with _____ (you fill in the number) qualified HNW prospects each week. To do that, you must first find HNW prospects that meet your *Ideal Client Profile* criteria. The activities necessary to achieve that goal fall into three categories.

1. Determine your HNW market niche.
2. Identify qualified prospects.
3. Find qualified prospects.

The remainder of this chapter will focus on preparing you to implement these activities.

Determine Your HNW Market Niche

Review your *Ideal Client Profile*. At this point, you should have established a minimum investable amount that you will require to open an account. It's probably somewhere between $250,000 and $10 million.

You may have a lower amount set now, with a higher amount targeted as you become more established in the HNW segment of the investor market. View that lower amount strictly as a "fall-back," the amount you will accept when you find a prospective client that you believe has future potential or a circle of influence you want to tap. As for your prospecting activity, focus all of your HNW prospecting efforts toward finding prospects that match your *Ideal Client Profile* criteria, including the minimum investable amount that you have set.

Rarely will you know precisely what a prospect has or is willing to invest with you when you first connect with them. However, you do want to know that they can bring serious money to the table. One way to do that is by focusing on individuals who fall within one of the *wealth categories*. Use the following criteria to select the category that provides the best arena of opportunity for you.

- Your background — Where you have worked and the knowledge and skills you have acquired.
- Your circle of influence — Your clients, family, friends, and acquaintances.
- Your areas of financial specialty.
- Clients and others you know who could serve as an *internal advocate* to help you penetrate your niche and introduce and refer you to the right people.

Once you select a category, the more you can learn about HNW people within that niche, the better.

- What professional and civic organizations they join.
- The causes they support.
- The watering holes they frequent.
- Unique ways they do business.

Here are brief descriptions of **10 general HNW categories**. Within each are subcategories which may enable you to select a narrower focus.

Generators of Wealth

1. *Entrepreneurs* – Their income and net worth will vary significantly. The top 10% dominate the market. Look for entrepreneurs who have

successfully created a growing business, have been in business at least 10 years, and are 50 plus years or older. Franchise owners are not technically "start-ups," but they are also a possibility.

2. *Self-employed professionals* – This includes medical professionals, attorneys, consultants, engineers, airline pilots, architects, coaches, chefs, etc. Their business typically has little value when it is time to retire, so they need to establish and wisely fund their own retirement plan rather than depend on the sale of their businesses.

3. *Artists and entertainers* – Some make huge incomes; others make a good steady living. Their agents tend to act as gatekeepers, making them hard to reach. Many of the younger prospects in this category have flamboyant and unstable lifestyles.

4. *Professional athletes* – The number of professional athletes and the salaries they receive make this a fast-growing industry. However, the serious money comes from personal appearances and product endorsements. A big challenge is the young age of most athletes and their relatively short careers. You also must deal with agents, lawyers, and managers who act as gatekeepers. In fact, these gatekeepers are often the only doorway to the athlete.

Earners of Wealth

5. *Key corporate employees* – This includes executives, managers, professionals, and skilled technicians. Since they are usually taken care of by their companies, the best time to approach these folks is when they are changing jobs or about to retire. The biggest opportunity is with those who, in addition to their retirement plan, own stock options in fast-growth companies.

6. *Salespeople (mainly commissioned)* – They are often overlooked by financial planners, yet the best salespeople make well over $100,000 a year.

Receivers of Wealth

7. *Retirees* – Approximately 33 million baby boomers will soon retire,

adding to the 30 million people currently over age 65. Many retirees are struggling financially, yet there are others who represent a very profitable target for financial advisors.

8. *Divorced women* – About 1.2 million divorces occur each year. In the top 5-10% of the most financially successful marriages, the wife typically gets all the liquid assets and the house, leaving the business-related assets to her husband. A spouse in this situation is often called "out spouse" because her support comes primarily from *his* attorney, accountant, investment advisor, and insurance agent. Divorcees, with all those assets but no personal advisor, provide a wide-open opportunity for you.

9. *Widows* – Women live an average of 7 years longer than their husbands. Around 650,000 women are widowed yearly. In many cases, they must suddenly take over all financial duties. What they usually want is to simplify everything, consolidate, and ensure that wills and estate plans are in order. Estate planning attorneys are good doorways.

10. *Inheritors* – The largest ever transfer of generational wealth, involving $10-$15 *trillion* in assets, will take place during the next 20 years. It is especially important to build relationships with your clients' children, especially if those children are over age 50. Estate planning professionals are also good doorways.

Whichever category or subcategory you select as your HNW market niche, that niche must provide you with two things:

- A substantial, and hopefully growing, potential client base.
- Access to those potential clients.

When it comes to niche marketing success stories, there are simply too many to share all of them with you. However, one stands out because it is so pure and compelling.

Maureen, in her own words, is a former "stockbroker." Her entrée into a unique niche came at the prodding of a client who was caught in the midst of an ugly divorce from her husband, and crying for help. Wanting very much to help, Maureen set out to educate herself on divorce planning.

She contacted the College for Financial Planning branch in Denver, discovered they had a Certified Divorce Specialist designation, and enrolled. That was the first step. Being exposed to her client's emotional roller-coaster, Maureen decided she also needed to have a better understanding of divorce proceedings. With permission from her client's attorney, she sat through every aspect of the court proceedings.

Fast-forward three years. Not only is Maureen now a Certified Divorce Specialist; she's an "expert witness," and charges thousands of dollars to advise divorce attorneys and their clients. Naturally, she becomes their go-to financial quarterback when the divorce is settled. Maureen's practice is magnetic. All of her business comes from referrals, and she dominates this unique HNW niche.

Developing strong expertise within a narrowly defined HNW niche is an effective way to minimize competition. Maureen is a good example of that.

Identify Qualified Prospects

Qualified in this case simply means you have identified a person and a valid reason to believe they are a prospective HNW client. The fact that an individual falls within your selected HNW market niche might be all the reason you need. Those prospects bring some serious money issues to the table, and they know it. However, accessing HNW people can be a challenge. You should look for those situations where you are convinced that your opportunity is greatest.

In a survey conducted for Quicken and reported in the *New York Times* in early 2003, 70% of high-income investors said their faith in financial experts had declined during the past year. In fact, only 30% of the respondents said they would continue consulting their stockbrokers on investment decisions. This indicates serious dissatisfaction, and as we noted earlier, dissatisfaction is the breeding ground of opportunity.

Most people do not like to dwell on dissatisfaction. Something must trigger those thoughts. Dissatisfaction with past financial advice tends to surface when HNW investors are in the midst of, or are about to experience, a significant **financial transition**. For example:

- Selling their business or professional practice.
- Exercising stock options.
- Taking their business public.
- Making a major reinvestment decision because a large bond has matured.
- Making a major investment decision because of dissatisfaction with their current portfolio.
- Wanting to reallocate their portfolio investment mix.
- Preparing to retire.
- Selling a large capital asset.
- Receiving or instituting a wealth transfer.
- Facing divorce.
- Signing a BIG contract.
- Wanting to change financial advisors.

Your greatest opportunity to connect with a qualified HNW prospect is to find someone in your niche who is *in transition* – and then listen carefully for one of the following **financial impact points**.

- An *uncomfortable condition* (on-going) – e.g., expressing concern over stock market fluctuations and the impact it is having or will have on their portfolio.
- An *uncomfortable situation* (isolated) – e.g. expressing concern about deciding where to reinvest a bond that is about to mature.
- A *problem* they want solved – e.g., facing a tax burden they didn't expect.
- An *improvement* they want right now – e.g., wanting a better financial advisor who will serve them as expected.

Barry's situation illustrates how important it is to act with confidence and clarity under pressure.

Barry had been referred by an attorney to an entrepreneur who had made millions in a franchise business and was considering going public. His first comment to Barry was to the point: "I just blew off the third call this month from my son-in-law stockbroker. I'm going to ask you exactly what I asked him, 'What sets you apart from everyone else who wants to advise me on my finances? Tell me why I should listen to you.'"

Without missing a beat, Barry responded that his expertise was in handling the wealth management complexities of HNW clients. Barry then provided an example of how helping a HNW client with the reallocation of his assets saved that client millions. He followed that with a question about the entrepreneur's business.

The HNW prospect enjoyed discussing his business success and mentioned his apprehension about going public. Recognizing the financial impact this represented, Barry began probing and providing illustrations of clients who had similar situations. Finally, Barry suggested this HNW prospect think long and hard about going public, explaining that he didn't need the cash for expansion and already had what the prospect had referred to as a "cash cow." Barry then explained that if the entrepreneur were to become his client, they would work on establishing long-term financial goals and a portfolio allocation strategy to achieve those goals. That, Barry explained, would provide the entrepreneur with a foundation to guide his investment decisions – and a financial advisor who understood what he was attempting to accomplish long-term. Knowing that HNW investors question the objectivity of the advice given by commission-based brokers, Barry also explained that he worked strictly on a fee basis.

Within three weeks, Barry not only had a new $20 million client, but also $70 million of additional assets in his pipeline. He had been introduced by the entrepreneur to the new client's top 10 franchisees, each of whom was earning in excess of 2 million dollars a year.

Let's analyze how this happened. Barry seized the referral opportunity, knowing that the entrepreneur's contemplated *financial transition* of going public could provide a window of opportunity. This was more than simply a referral to a HNW individual; the encounter quickly revealed two *financial impact points*. The entrepreneur wanted to replace his "son-in-law stockbroker," and he was apprehensive about taking his business public. Barry's astute response to both needs created immediate professional respect, a new HNW client, and a HNW referral source. And Barry was savvy enough to anticipate a potential concern about the lack of objectivity with broker commissions.

You cannot expect to always duplicate Barry's success, but whenever a HNW investor is facing a *financial transition*, you have an opportunity to probe for key *financial impact points* that will enable you to differentiate yourself from your competition. Uncovering the *financial impact points* that typically exist during *financial transitions* enables you to avoid simply listing your services and immediately demonstrates your potential value. That's important because *value* is exactly what HNW prospects want.

Find Qualified Prospects

Once you know your niche and the importance of looking for HNW prospects "in transition," the question is, "How do you find them?" It's easy to gather names, but discovering a good reason to initiate contact is the challenge. The reason will largely be determined by the methods you use to find your HNW prospects. Here are your options:

1. Word-Of-Mouth Influence (WOMI)

There is no better way to uncover names (with good reasons to make contact) than through word-of-mouth influence. People who provide those names know you and what you do, so they are likely to provide names of people they believe you can help, and will tell you why they are suggesting them.

Personal introductions provide the strongest contact, but if that is not possible, ask for a referral. Later, when you make your first contact with a prospect referred to you, mentioning the person who referred you will create instant credibility. Your two best WOMI sources are …

- Key clients who are in your HNW market niche, and who are on good terms with others in that category.

- Family, their friends, and your friends who are in (or who know those who are in) your HNW market niche.

The best way to gain introductions and referrals is to simply ask for them.

As you know, my business is built entirely through word of mouth. We have known each other [been working together] for some time, and I wonder ... do you know anyone who might need the kinds of financial solutions I have been providing [for you]?

(As a matter of fact, I do). *Is there any way we could arrange a convenient introduction?*

If an introduction is not convenient:

Would you be agreeable to my using your name when I call for an appointment?

(Yes, that would be fine).

And if, but only if, you believe it's appropriate:

Would you be willing to contact those people in advance to let them know you have given me their names – and to explain some of the ways you feel they might benefit from meeting with me?

Or, you can use the following technique that Barry used with his HNW entrepreneur client in the example above, the one that resulted in 10 HNW personal introductions!

I think there might be some value for me to get in front of your top franchise owners and take a look at how their portfolios are being allocated and managed. Could you help me organize this?

2. Networking

You should always be networking and ready to talk with anyone who shows any sign of interest. In some social settings, "doing business" may not be appropriate, but you can be guided by the interest expressed by the other person. These opportunities will generally come when you have been sharing a story about how you helped someone solve a financial need. When you notice they are interested and are impressed with your story, you can say ...

(Name), my business is built entirely through word of mouth. You now have an idea of some of the work I do ... do you know anyone who is at a point where he or she might need the kinds of financial solutions I can provide?

(As a matter of fact, I do). *Would you be agreeable to my using your name when I contact them for a possible appointment?*

(Yes, that would be fine).

3. Referral Alliances

Referral Alliances are a proactive means of tapping into a non-client's personal and business-related centers of influence. Not all referrals need come from satisfied clients. Many can come through alliances you create with individuals who may never become your client. These alliances should be with professionals who provide complementary, but non-competitive, products and services to the HNW people you wish to contact.

Prepare yourself! This is a "give and take" approach. You must be ready and willing to use any opportunity to give referrals to those you add to your alliance. Providing referrals is a *deliberate act*, not an accidental one. Here are a few pointers:

- Try to give a referral before asking for one.
- Get permission before referring someone. You'll avoid uncomfortable situations that may derail your alliance efforts.
- Have good, accurate information about anyone you refer to your alliance partners. Be clear about why you are referring them.
- Update that information periodically.
- Don't sit on hot referrals. Pass them on quickly.

- Don't give the same referral to more than 1 or 2 non-competing alliance partners.

- Don't get caught up in schemes (e.g., splitting fees) that may be illegal or violate company policy.

Create your alliance by targeting professionals you trust and know have good reputations. Make certain they "cross the path" of the people you are targeting, and that they provide products or services that are complementary and comparable in quality to those you provide.

Gather the names of the top CPAs and attorneys in your community. Start by asking your top clients for the names of those they would recommend. Call the individuals referred to you and say:

My name is _____. I'm a financial / investment advisor (or whatever label you use) *with _____. I was told by _____ that you do an excellent job for your clients. I have a number of clients who may need tax/legal advice in the future, and I think there may be some mutual benefit to our meeting and talking about ways we might refer business to each other.*

Invite the CPA or attorney to lunch or a meeting in 1 to 2 weeks to see if you can establish a Referral Alliance.

Send potential allies a packet of materials, including your biographical information, to look over before you meet. You might request similar information from them.

Proceed carefully during your first meeting.

- First, establish ground rules for referring them. Ask them to define their *Ideal Client Profile* so they will know you are eager to help them effectively build their businesses through the referrals you give them.

- Determine the procedure you will follow for providing them with a referral. Then reverse the process. Review your *Ideal Client Profile* with them, and work with them to establish ground rules for giving you referrals. They will likely follow your example.

- Agree to try the arrangement for 30, 60, or 90 days. Then meet to work out any bugs.

Approach this alliance as you would any professional relationship. Honor your commitments, serve the other person well, and add value whenever possible. By adopting a "give before you get" attitude, you will be surprised at how well a Referral Alliance can pay dividends.

In summary, there are four keys to make your Referral Alliance strategy work:

- Serve your clients, Referral Alliances and referred prospects, well. Provide true value that exceeds their expectations. Nurture relationships of trust.

- Be clear about your *Ideal Client Profile*. Constantly plant referral seeds, and continuously ask for introductions and referrals.

- Become known for building your business exclusively through introductions and referrals. Be assertive, but not overly aggressive. Ask for help, and treat such requests with respect. Do not only ask for introductions and referrals; give them as well.

- After you contact a referral, inform the person who provided the referral, and express your thanks. If feasible, share the outcome of that contact.

4. Researching Publications

We will use "publications" as a general term that includes business directories, newspaper articles, TV news stories, membership directories, etc. To be most useful, you need to select what you will research, when you will do it, and what you expect to find there.

Newspapers, business journals, and local TV are especially useful for finding information about HNW people who are "in transition." Their status in the community makes those transitions newsworthy. When you find such an article or news story, you not only have someone to contact, but also an up-to-the-minute reason for doing so.

Pipeline "Tips"

Following are two PIPELINE TIPS that could change your prospecting habits forever. Both require going back to basics and the use of a notebook.

Label one notebook as your **Top 25 Client Referral List**. As you talk with each of your top 25 clients, orchestrate the conversation toward uncovering the names of colleagues, golfing buddies, neighbors, family members, and other acquaintances. Write those names in your notebook, and then add a few comments about each new name, particularly any reasons why they might be a qualified prospect. At some future date, ask for an introduction or referral to these individuals. Financial professionals who use this technique swear that it is 100% effective.

As an example, suppose you've done your homework and determined that your Top 25 client Jack plays golf with Matt Oechsli. A few weeks after you uncover this gem, you call Top 25 client Jack, engage in some small talk (if there is nothing professional to discuss), and than boldly ask:

"I'd like to meet your golfing buddy, Matt Oechsli. How about setting-up a round of golf — on me?"

Do not assume that your Top 25 client will be able to accurately articulate your value when you, your Top 25 client, and your new HNW prospect all get together. The safest bet is to clarify with your client what you really do, and what you would like your client to say when the introduction is made.

"As you know, Jack, we really focus our practice on a select clientele. We handle every aspect of our clients' financial affairs, from minimizing taxes, to generational planning, gifting, investments, and so on. But when you introduce me to Matt Oechsli at the golf club, rather than describe all of that, just tell him that I'm a partner in a financial practice that handles financial affairs for a select clientele, and that I personally handle your affairs."

Since each client has his or her own personality and a unique relationship with you, this scripting should be adjusted as necessary for each situation. If you skip this preparatory step, you run the risk of being introduced as a stockbroker, insurance agent, financial planner, or a similar title. While there is nothing wrong with these professions, most HNW prospects have a preconceived notion of what these labels represent – sales. So don't be shy about explaining the role you would like your Top 25 client to play. You will be pleasantly surprised at how closely they will follow your script. HNW clients love to help, and they understand the value of word-of-mouth influence. They simply need to be asked, and guided.

- Label another notebook your **Master Dream List**. In this notebook, list every individual or entity that you would love to have as a client. As with your other notebook, you will want to include some personal information about each name — including who could introduce you.

Some financial advisors are uneasy about developing a Master Dream List. "I don't know many people with money" is the common 'knee-jerk' reaction. This may be true, but it is also the reason why a Master Dream List works so well.

Because most financial advisors are not accustomed to marketing to the affluent, their first list is usually rather sparse. The key is to start with who you now know, and then keep adding names. You'll be surprised at how quickly the list expands.

Veteran stockbrokers Lee and Fred are a perfect example. They recently joined forces to form a Wealth Management Team. Their initial effort to create a Master Dream List resulted in only seven HNW names. They were very disappointed and immediately said, "Forget that," but I couldn't let them give up so easily. My role was to keep them on their Critical Path, performing their HNW Selling Process activities every day. Since they came up with seven names today, I suggested they add seven more tomorrow – and the next day – and again the next day.

What did adding seven names a day do for Lee and Fred? In their first 12 months, they surpassed everyone's expectations – and especially their own. Within three years, they increased their assets by over 250 million dollars.

Somewhere during that third year, their firm asked me to conduct a Wealth Management Team workshop. Lee and Fred attended. When I directed everyone to compile their Master Dream List, I noticed Lee was already writing. So I asked, "Lee, how many names do you have so far?" Turning a light shade of red, he did a quick count and answered, "63". I then asked, "Could you estimate the asset total represented by these names?" The silence was noticeable as everyone anxiously awaited Lee's calculations. "Gosh, there's over one billion dollars on this list," he replied.

I asked Lee if he remembered how many names he and Fred had written on their original Master Dream List three years ago. He thought the number was five, and then he commented on how they had gone from that disappointing moment to where they are today.

Lee also emphasized that a list of names isn't what makes you successful. He proudly announced that either he or Fred will attempt to get face-to-face with everyone on this new list within the next three years. He predicted that they should be able to conduct business with 75 percent of those individuals. That's about 48 new HNW clients.

Lee and Fred have become masters at doing their homework and obtaining introductions to the names on their Master Dream List. This list has become an important tool for keeping them on their Critical Path. If you will do the same, the results of your efforts will be compounded in ways that you cannot predict.

System implies systematic. The effort to find qualified HNW prospects must be done systematically. However, no system is going to drive your efforts without a clear purpose that you believe is vital to your success. The purpose behind your HNW prospecting system is to fill your pipeline with qualified HNW prospects. You now know how to find them. Once you find them, your challenge is to schedule quality face time with them. In the next chapter, we will provide you with techniques to do that.

5
Filling Your Pipeline

The primary goal of your Critical Path activity is to keep your pipeline full of HNW prospects. Contacting qualified prospects to schedule face time is where it all begins. This is also the area where many experience the *social self-consciousness* challenge discussed in Chapter 2.

Absolutely, the best way to overcome your face-to-face resistance is to "just do it." As you find qualified prospects (the easy part), contact them without delay. Schedule contact activities daily, and follow through without fail. Now that you know how to find qualified prospects, you have no valid reason to procrastinate.

Let me make a very important point here. This is not *cold calling* in the traditional sense, and you are probably relieved to know that. Here's a clever method that illustrates why cold calling is distasteful for so many. Let's say you want to contact the Benefits Manager of a major corporation, but you don't have a name. You call and ask to speak to Matt Oechsli. The receptionist responds, "Who? There's no Matt Oechsli here." You say, "Matt Oechsli – your Benefits Manager." The receptionist then says, "No, that's not the right person. It's Benny Fits. He's our Benefits Manager." You reply, "Oh, I'm sorry. I have the wrong name. Let me change my records. Is Mr. Fits in?" You cold call hoping to find a reason to meet with someone, anyone.

Fortunately, you don't have to call to get the name of Benny Fits so you can try to sell him a 401K. You have learned ways to not only uncover HNW investor names, but also a reason to contact each individual you call. Armed with that information, you can focus on using any (probably all) of the following five methods for making contact with HNW prospects.

A. **Introductions** – In each of the first two options for finding prospects in Chapter 4, the people you are talking with are what we call *Internal Advocates*. They have contacts inside a HNW market niche that you want to reach, and you are asking them to be an advocate for you with individuals in that niche. Advocates include those individuals you have connected with through Word of Mouth Influence (WOMI), Networking, and Referral Alliances.

When someone identifies an individual and a reason you should contact them, the next step is to ask for an introduction. Suggest a breakfast or lunch appointment, whichever they prefer (you pick up the tab). Your conversation might go something like this.

> *It's certainly important that I get to know* (name)*, but it's even more important that they get to know me. Since you know both of us, your presence at our first meeting will be a big help. It would be great if we could meet with* (name) *for either breakfast or lunch at a convenient time next* (week, specific day)*. Would you be willing to set that up?*

B. Phone Call with a Referral – If your HNW client is not able or willing to arrange an introduction for you, it's likely that they will give you a referral. As noted earlier, there are two things you should ask when requesting a referral.

- Why is your client giving you this name? Is there a particular problem? Is there something you offer that the referrer feels this person needs? Do they believe the prospect would be open to talking with you about that issue?

- IS your client willing to call the prospect first and endorse you – and let the prospect know you will be calling?

When you call a person who was referred to you, keep in mind that upfront social conversation can be a turnoff. Think of how you react when a telemarketer calls you, asks for you by name, then says, "How are you today?" Immediately, you suspect they want to sell you something. In contrast, you were referred to them, and you have a reason to contact them. If the person who referred you has already phoned them and endorsed you, this call will be a snap!

Start by stating your name, and who gave you their name. Explain exactly why you are calling – to have a chance to meet them. Here's an example:

Good morning. This is [your name]. [Name of person who referred you] *suggested that I give you a call, and I promised I would.*

The reason I'm calling is [give reason].

Could we get together for [breakfast, lunch, etc.] *next Thursday?*

Don't provide any more information unless specifically asked. The entire conversation should last no longer than a minute or two. Your objective is to arrange a face-to-face contact, nothing more. This is your first mini-close, and you are handling it in such an inoffensive manner that it is very difficult for this HNW referral to refuse. If for some reason you are turned down, it is obviously not the right time, or they did not have a strong enough reason to accept.

Always leave the door open. You have a HNW prospect name, and you believe that you have a good reason to call them. Their dissatisfaction with their present situation may grow, and other reasons may emerge. Keep checking back with the person who referred you to find another time and reason to pick up the phone and call.

C. **Phone Call Without a Referral** – These contacts are from your research of publications and other media where you were looking for HNW individuals and reasons to contact them. Because you have found a reason to make contact, making this call won't be as difficult as a traditional cold call. We call this a *warm call*. However, it's important that you develop a custom script for each call you make. Here's a format you can follow:

Good morning (their name). *This is* (your name) *of* (your firm) *here in* (your town).

I noticed in (source) *that* (the reason you are calling). *It caught my attention because we* (link to what you do, or something specific you did for a client).

I'm calling to ask for an appointment so we can explore a potential match between your financial management needs and our services.

Would breakfast (or lunch) next (day) work for you?

The second paragraph is the key. How you present the publication source, your reason for calling, and the link to what you do will largely determine your success in getting face time with serious money prospects. After you've created a script for a specific call, run it by trusted colleagues. In time, it will become second nature. Here is an example to help you see the possibilities.

> *I noticed in the* **paper last night** *that* **you are about to sell your business and retire** (a key wealth management need). *It caught my attention because we* **have been able to help several clients in your situation avoid the tax and other risks that often occur**.

D. Targeted and Exclusive Seminars – As we discussed at the beginning of this chapter, it is difficult to get HNW investors to attend a typical financial seminar when they suspect it is primarily a sales gimmick. However, it can work when your seminar is targeted to a specific area of need or dissatisfaction, and it's an exclusive (and genuine) "by invitation only" affair.

Your ability to offer successful targeted and exclusive seminars to HNW prospects will be the direct result of having a well-planned, high priority and systematic prospecting system. Over time, you will be able to identify clusters of need and dissatisfaction. Every method for finding qualified HNW prospects will provide you with a list of names and reasons to contact them. Not only that, you can team up with others who are using this same system and offer a joint seminar. You simply agree that each prospect remains with the person who invited them.

Here are some guidelines to help you plan an appropriate event.

- "Appropriate" is especially important to keep in mind here, because HNW prospects are not eager to attend another meeting.

- *Never* invite HNW prospects to a seminar with a hidden agenda which will be presented only after they arrive. Instead, create a seminar benefit statement and incorporate it into your invitation.

• Incorporate adequate time for interacting with and answering questions from those attending. People love talking about themselves, and your HNW prospects will be impressed with your efforts to understand them better. This also provides an opportunity for your entire team to interact with the attendees, which enhances team member understanding and helps cement their relationship with each individual.

We often think of a seminar as a single point of contact, to be followed up with one or more additional contacts. Actually, there are **seven contact points** which provide rich opportunities to connect with HNW prospects before, during, and after the seminar.

1. The **initial phone call** to invite prospects to attend. That's *phone call* — not a printed or written invitation. Call and explain why you are inviting them, to show that you are in touch with their needs and are taking steps to serve them.

2. The **confirmation letter** you send to those who accept. Begin by confirming why you invited them, and note anything pertinent they said when accepting when you initially called to invite them. Then provide the what, who, where, and when details.

3. The **reminder phone call** 2 or 3 days before the seminar. After your prospect's attendance is confirmed, ask if there is anything specific they would like covered, or any questions they would like answered during the seminar. When you pass on that information to the presenter, make absolutely certain it will be incorporated into the seminar format.

4. The **informal reception** before the seminar begins. Plan this time carefully so you or one of your staff is able to personally greet and welcome every participant. If someone reaches their seat before that happens, go over and have a brief conversation with them.

5. The **seminar program** itself. When you incorporate your HNW prospects' interests and questions into the program, important connections are made. Make certain the seminar is interactive and allows questions at appropriate points, rather than simply at the end.

6. The **informal time immediately following** the presentation. Be sure to have your appointment book with you. Take advantage of the *emotional moment* to set up follow-up appointments with everyone. Since participants were invited because of their interests and needs, they will be expecting that follow-up effort. Don't disappoint them! Provide refreshments, make certain everyone knows there is no rush to leave, and see everyone before they go — without exception. You and all your staff should stay until after the last guest leaves.

7. The **follow-up phone call** 1 or 2 days later to confirm the follow-up appointment. Personalize each call by referring back to something they said during or following the presentation, and express your eagerness to meet with them.

It takes considerable time, effort, and cost to plan and execute an effective, targeted seminar for HNW prospects. However, the payoff will make everything you did worth the effort.

Mark's Wealth Management Team was leading his region in seminar attendance and glowing evaluations. He was becoming known as the guru of seminars. Mark loved speaking in front of groups.

Living in a wealthy retirement community, his team would send out invitations to attend a luncheon at a posh resort in the area. They averaged 30 attendees. Mark would give his presentation, his team would collect the evaluation forms (which were always glowing), and then they would spend the next two weeks calling attendees to set appointments.

In addition to this being laborious, they were not getting enough appointments to justify their efforts. Equally important, the ones they were getting frequently did not qualify as HNW prospects. But because they were able to get funding from a mutual fund company, and Mark loved to present, they continued to hold seminars. In fact, it eventually became their only marketing vehicle.

I met Mark following a HNW Selling workshop. After listening to him explain his seminar process, I asked how many new HNW clients that fit his ideal Client Profile had he attracted over the past 12 months. He wasn't sure. I asked how often he asked for referrals or used word-of-mouth influence. He confessed that they were "not very strong" in that arena.

It was clear that by tweaking three basic aspects of Mark's HNW prospecting initiative, his results could change dramatically. First, rather than looking for glowing evaluations, Mark agreed to sell the attendees on a free hour of his time and schedule an appointment before they left. Any follow-up phone calls would be only to confirm the appointment.

Second, instead of using these seminars as his only HNW marketing activity, Mark and his two associates agreed to do at least one of the following every day: Meet with one HNW prospect or one center-of-influence, and ask for a HNW introduction or referral.

Third, Mark and his associates agreed to change their tracking mechanism so they would focus on HNW face-to-face contacts and assets in the pipeline rather than seminar presentation evaluations.

Mark's team was able to increase their new HNW clients fourfold within six months. They continued to hold seminars, but quarterly rather than twice a month. Most significant, they were averaging eight appointments per engagement, all with HNW prospects who were now the target of their seminars. The significant increase in other prospecting efforts helped Mark's team identify the topics of greatest interest to HNW prospects.

Tony, a successful seminar practitioner in the Midwest, provided another successful seminar technique which can enable you to continue building your HNW prospecting list. Of the many good techniques Tony shared, two put a smile on my face. He writes *Free Lunch at XYC* on the outside of the envelope. This ensures a higher percentage will open the mail. Secondly, at the conclusion of the

seminar, he holds a raffle for an inexpensive Palm Pilot. The requirement to participate is to fill out a short form with the attendee's information, plus list a HNW friend or associate who could be invited to
the next seminar. According to Tony, everyone participates in the raffle.

E. Place Yourself in Their Path

I read recently that in major cities, every CEO in town takes an elevator at one time or another. If you spend 1-2 hours a day riding up
and down select elevators, you will come face-to-face with enough
CEOs to keep your pipeline full of qualified prospects. Elevator
prospecting may not sound enticing to you, but there is an important
principle here:

> **If you place yourself *in the path* of qualified HNW prospects
> every day, the results will exceed your expectations.**

Where can you go to place yourself in the path of qualified HNW
prospects?

Write your answers to each of the following questions on a legal pad.

1. Where do my best clients in my HNW market niche network?
2. What three professional and civic organizations should I investi-
   gate and possibly join?
3. Who are the five prime people in my HNW market niche that I
   want to meet?
4. What upcoming events might those five people attend?
5. What watering holes do those five people frequent?
6. What causes do those five people support?

In Chapter 4, you were introduced to Tim, a 20-year veteran struggling with the transition to become a *go-to HNW financial quarterback*. As Tim began to consider what he needed to do, he quickly
thought of an answer to the "where do they network" question. Part
of Tim's efforts to 'skate to the money' led him to join a health club
catering to HNW self-employed professionals he had targeted. In
return, that led to 9 million dollars in his pipeline with 4 million
closed rather quickly.

There are two advantages gained from adding this strategy to your prospecting system. First, you will meet and talk with the people you want to service. Second, you will become more aware of their habits and become more comfortable in their presence. This would be especially helpful if you struggle with *social self-consciousness.*

When you have a list of places to go with dates when you should be there, view them as **Networking Events** – and enter each event in your day planner. Preparation for each event is vital to your success. Here's what you should do.

- **Plan your involvement at the event**. Determine who will be there, what your objectives will be, and what you need to take.

- **Show up early**. Arrive ready to network, and stop at the entrance to plan your first move.

- **Walk the area at least twice**. Become familiar with the room and who is there.

- **Stay alert.** Eat early, don't drink, and don't smoke.

- **Spend at least 75% of your time with people you don't know**. Resist the temptation to escape with someone you know.

- **Target those you want to meet**. Identify 3 to 6 people.

- **Approach, smile, and shake hands firmly**. Show warmth and display confidence.

- **Say their name at least twice**. First, to help you remember it. Second, because it is the most pleasing word to their ears.

- **Tell them your name and what you do**. Briefly — very briefly. Help them help you by giving them only enough to encourage them to ask questions.

- **Exchange cards**. You want their name, etc. – and you want to help them know you better.

- **Ask them something to get them talking about themselves**. At an event, ask "What brings you here tonight (today)?" This is a great start.

- **Keep asking questions to get them to tell you more about themselves, and then about their business endeavors.** Keep probing.

- **Listen for financial transitions and areas of possible dissatisfaction**. This is where you can say you specialize in that area and suggest breakfast or lunch on (day) to see if there is a way you might be able to help them.

This entire process is geared to get you appointments with qualified HNW prospects. If you schedule 3-6 hours of activities per week to place yourself in the path of qualified prospects, you will never have to worry about finding your next client.

Activity drives the dream. In order to effectively fill your HNW Pipeline, you must do the right activity, the right way, directed toward the right person. That's what the concept of *Critical Path* is all about. Everything boils down to getting face-to-face with HNW prospects and centers of influence, including existing HNW clients. To realize the importance of this, think of one face-to-face with a HNW client, center of influence, or prospect each day as being the equivalent of 300 "cold call" phone dials during those days when the market was growing steadily and you weren't targeting HNW prospects.

Everett has now mastered the HNW Selling process. To do so, he first had to learn a hard lesson. He had become lazy because, in his mind, he had little if any competition. He wasn't bothered by social self-confidence. He could pick up the phone and call any HNW prospect with ease, or so he thought.

One of his clients belonged to the most prestigious country club in the Northeast. Everyone of wealth and prominence was a member. Everett pestered his client for three years to get a copy of the club membership directory. With those names and numbers, all he had to do was pick up the phone, or so he thought. Here's how he explained his great awakening.

"I was foolish enough to think that I had just received a book of gold, when in reality, I didn't have a clue as to the proper way to use it," he explained. "After the first couple of telephone calls, I quickly learned that I needed more than a name and number to get anywhere. Fortunately, I stopped after the third call.

I learned the hard way that introductions and referrals work best for me. From that point forward, whenever I'd visit my client, I'd ask him to introduce me to one of the members I'd identified and researched. As my HNW client base expanded, I continued that approach."

Filling your pipeline must become a series of planned activities. Now that you know what those activities should be, make your choices, create your prospecting plan, and plug everything into your daily planner. After you have planned what to do, make certain you do what you planned!

Scheduling face-to-face meetings with qualified HNW prospects will give you the momentum you need to move along the Critical Path to the next phase.

Getting Face-To-Face with HNW Prospects

Chapter 6

Helping Them KNOW You

Chapter 7

Helping Them LIKE You

Chapter 8

Getting Them to TRUST You

6

Helping Them KNOW You

The final thought in the last chapter is worth repeating, so I will. Getting face-to-face with qualified prospects is what will launch your *HNW Selling Process*. Whether it's a casual encounter, a scheduled meeting, or a planned social event, the only right way to initiate true HNW prospecting is face-to-face.

Before we go any further, I want to explain why *face-to-face* communication is given such strong emphasis in this book. It is actually a term communication experts use, and they typically emphasize two things. First, it's the *richest* medium of communication possible. Second, it's becoming a lost art as we place more and more emphasis on technology and the gadgets of telecommunication.

Rich communication is especially important in the early stages when the emotional decision to work with you is being made. In preparation for face-to-face meetings, the focus is typically on language. We believe that if we can get those words and phrases just right, our message will be communicated effectively. It's true that language is an important tool for expressing ideas and concepts, but there are some things that language simply cannot convey. In fact, verbal language only accounts for about 7% of what we communicate. The other 93% is divided between how we sound (38%) and how we look (55%); better known as non-verbal communication.

Face-to-face communication allows non-verbal expression, which often says more than words alone can express:

- Facial expression and eye movements.
- Body language and posture.
- How you dress.
- The physical distance between you and the other person.
- Responding by nodding your head and making gestures.

- Short response utterances such as "OK", "yes", or "aha."
- Hand movements to express action or point to something.

As obvious as non-verbal cues seem, we use them without thinking, and others absorb them without realizing it. They help to connect us to each other. In fact, we like to communicate so much that we can actually create over 10,000 different facial expressions. Here are some examples: a single nod of the head indicates that you understand; while you are speaking, rapid and repeated head nods by the other person are a signal that they wish to speak; we underline points by raising our eyebrows or pursing our lips. Facial expression makes the language we use so much richer. Because we can all lip-read to some extent, we typically spend 75% of the time watching the other person speak.

It isn't that form has more impact than substance, but in the HNW prospecting game of face-to-face contact, form and substance must be consistent. HNW prospects watch to see if you are genuine. If you don't get the form right, you won't need to be concerned about substance. Your HNW prospects will tune out and stop listening to your words. Remember, HNW prospects fear salespeople almost as much as they despise paying taxes.

One final tip — there is nothing as powerful as a smile to make an emotional impact. Research indicates that the muscular action of smiling appears to release serotonin (a key chemical for keeping us happy) in the brain. A genuine smile of enjoyment not only makes us feel good; it makes those around us feel good. It all starts with the eyes. Try it, and you'll 'see' what I mean.

You're Face-To-Face. Now What?

Frequently, your first face-to-face encounter with a HNW prospect will be scheduled in advance. Preparation is vital! "You don't have a second chance to make a first impression" may be an old cliché, but in this case *old* means tried and true. You essentially have about 3 minutes to make the right impression. Here's a preparation checklist:

The First 3 Minutes

- Get a good night's sleep the night before. You need to be refreshed, alert, and cheerful when you meet.
- Place anything you are carrying in your left hand, so you don't have to juggle it around to shake hands.
- Make certain you remember, and can pronounce, the person's name correctly, and with confidence.
- Smile! Think of something pleasant; then start smiling from your eyes. Relax your face. Make it natural.
- Extend your right hand naturally and begin a firm (but not viselike) handshake.
- Prepare a self-introduction ahead of time. It should include your name and a tag line that quickly tells them who you are. See examples below.
- Prepare for *small talk*. (See below.)

Your Self-Introduction

The purpose of a self-introduction is to remind this HNW prospect of who you are, and provide him or her with a pleasant first experience with you. You will want to use different self-introductions for different situations.

- If you want to highlight your company: "Hello, I'm John Doe with HNW Wealth Management Group."
- If you were referred by a client: "Hi, I'm John Doe. I handle the financial affairs for Bill Thompson and his family."
- If you were referred by a mutual friend: "Hi, I'm John Doe, a mutual friend of Mary Field."
- If you discovered a personal connection when you made the appointment: "Hello, I'm John Doe, your fellow Cole graduate from back in '92."

Your most powerful introduction is simply to smile, make good eye contact, give a firm handshake, state your name and refer to a common link (friend, profession, school, neighborhood, etc.). In the intangibles world, you are the product, regardless of the prestige of your company. Rather than allow your HNW prospect to jump to any conclusions about your professional value, you want to orchestrate the encounter so you will be asked the "What do you do for a living?" question. And because you are a professional, trained in the art and science of HNW Selling, you respond confidently:

"I handle the financial affairs for a select group of families."

With that or a similar brief statement, you can make an important positive first impression. You haven't said you are a stockbroker, or an insurance agent (or even a financial advisor) at XYZ firm. Instead, you have very briefly stated what you do for your clients – suggesting that you can do the same for them. Talk about non-verbal communication! Watch their eyebrows move slightly upward. You have peaked their curiosity and not allowed them to prematurely categorize you. This is a subtle point frequently lost on financial advisors, but is never lost on your HNW prospect.

At this stage, you must also be prepared for follow-up questions that will flow naturally from your statement.

Q. What do you mean by a "select" group of families?
A. Well our typical family has in the neighborhood of three to five million dollars to invest, and we act as their financial quarterback.

Q. What is a financial quarterback?
A. We function like a family CFO who makes certain that all aspects of our families' financial affairs are organized and working together. We help to minimize tax exposure, make investment decisions within their allotted risk tolerance, oversee the debt side of the ledger sheet, and keep their estate issues current. It's because our services are comprehensive and long-term that we are so selective.

Q. Well, it sounds great. How would I know if I qualify?
A. Let's meet together and take a look at your financial affairs. We normally can accomplish that within an hour. I suggest meeting next week. Is Wednesday afternoon or Friday morning better for you?

Such a meeting is obviously not the result of a cold call, but rather comes from an orchestrated social-networking affair. Nevertheless, it is well-planned, well-rehearsed, professionally delivered, and leads to a mini-close (a Wednesday afternoon or Friday morning meeting).

In other instances, you might not get that "What do you do?" question so early in the conversation. Therefore, you must also be skilled in developing rapport through the art of small talk.

Preparing For Small Talk

Deep down inside most of us think, "How do I start a conversation with a stranger, and an affluent one at that?" Since the purpose of small talk is to make the other person feel at ease and comfortable, you must avoid heavy subjects like politics and religion. If you were introduced or referred to them, ask the referrer to tell you anything personal about them that he or she thinks would be valuable for you to know. Don't assume they like what you like, and try to avoid the weather. Come to the meeting prepared with a statement or questions to get them talking about themselves and their interests.

Above all, keep your objective in mind – to help them *know you* as the first step in initiating a serious money relationship. Taking the right approach in those first three minutes will speak volumes. Remember Jay, the successful million dollar cold-caller who was able to make the transition to an even more successful financial advisor immersed in the HNW Sales Process? Here is how he combined form and substance for his face-to-face encounters.

> *"It took me about a week to get my act together before I felt prepared enough to get in front of my first HNW prospect, at least in my own mind. For me, two things were critical. First, was pulling together the specialists who could enable me to credibly sell myself as a professional ready to provide solutions for the multidimensional aspects of my HNW clientele's financial affairs. Second, was to master my HNW Selling process. I wrote out my lines, rehearsed them, re-wrote the ones that felt awkward, and rehearsed them again. I felt like Marlon Brando preparing to play The Godfather."*

Jay's HNW Selling Process was a customized version of what we are presenting in this book. In every face-to-face meeting, his first objective was to establish rapport. In order to succeed at this, he became a master of form. He told me that he was even teased by his peers for always "dressing for success." His body language, eye contact, and personal power were all carefully checked a few minutes before every initial encounter. Jay left nothing to chance. He became a master at showing a strong interest in each prospect and then getting them to talk about themselves. Within three to five minutes, he could usually steer the conversation toward that all-important "What do you do for a living?" question.

As you ponder Jay's experience, think about the phrase, *little things mean a lot.* I remember years ago, in my self-deluded arrogance, teasing my mother-in-law about a needle point she made saying "Little things mean a lot." Of course, she got the last laugh, because it has been a fixture in our house for over 20 years. Do not make my mistake and assume you already *are* paying attention to the little details. The odds are you are not, and that can make the difference between success and failure in HNW Selling.

What we have been discussing are some of the *little things* that make a huge difference in building rapport with HNW prospects. It was because Jay paid close attention to those details that he learned how to become successful in everything from chance meetings to carefully orchestrated social encounters.

You need to approach HNW face-to-face encounters with an open mind. Never assume that you have mastered the form and substance necessary to successfully sell up-market. Learn from every encounter.

Projecting The Right Image

Attitude is where image begins. You should not believe that HNW prospects are bigger than life, nor that they need you a lot more than you need them. The best relationships emerge when you need them *and* they need you. You are face-to-face to discover if you can find common ground.

Image begins with physical appearance. Here are some tips:

- If you're not sure whether to wear a suit, wear a suit. You can always take off your coat and place it on the back of your chair.

- Dark blue tends to inspire trust on a subconscious level. Black tends to project an air of authority, and is often not a good choice for a first meeting.

- Whatever you wear, make certain it is clean, pressed, and has no frayed cuffs or collars.

- Beards and mustaches unconsciously elicit distrust for many people.

- High-quality wool material, leather belts, and leather hard-soled shoes often create the impression that you handle lucrative accounts.

- If you are female, avoid a girlish or collegiate look and hairstyle, or any sexually suggestive attire.

- Avoid wearing several different colors together; it tends to diminish your professional appearance.

- Avoid excessive jewelry that draws attention to you (e.g., large rings, gold bracelets, large and expensive watches).

A common flaw when attempting to project the right image is trying too hard to impress. This can take many forms: being too friendly, talking too much, getting too personal, or even acting too confident. Darin learned this lesson the hard way.

As an understudy to a successful wealth manager, Darin quickly became the protégé. He was being groomed by the senior partner to handle his role when he was on vacation, with the implication that Darin would eventually take over the practice.

Darin spoke well, dressed for success, and was so photogenic his firm used him in a national advertising campaign. But he had a problem when he accompanied his senior partner to face-to-face meetings. In an attempt to disguise his inexperience, Darin would sit with his arms folded, lean back in his chair feigning disinterest, and speak with an air of know-it-all arrogance.

The senior partner had noticed Darin's posturing, but he wasn't aware it was a serious problem until a HNW prospect was escorting him back to his car. The prospect expressed some interest in working with his wealth management team. Then he added, "But, I don't want anything to do with Darin."

Darin dressed for success, but he failed to master the most important aspect of establishing rapport with a HNW prospect. By overcompensating for his insecurity, he projected a big ego and made the wrong impression.

We've talked about non-verbal cues, but language is also important, particularly the subtle messages you send. Here are some tips.

- Your vocabulary should be fluid and absent of technical terms. If you're concerned about your ability to sustain a fluid conversation, consider attending several Toastmaster meetings. Give special attention to impromptu speeches where you have to think on your feet. Another option is hiring a speech coach.

- Verbal content is also important. As noted earlier, avoid talk about politics, religion, or any other controversial topic. More important, don't "bad mouth" other individuals, your firm, or any other organization.

- Confidentiality must always be preserved. If you tell "stories," keep names and any other descriptions out that would enable them to identify people and situations. You've probably noticed that no last names are used in any of the "stories" I use. That's because my examples are all true and involve real financial advisors. Confidentiality is a must; I even changed the first names.

- Beware of being too talkative, a problem that can easily occur if you are nervous.

What They Need To Know About You

Your HNW prospect knows your name. He or she also knows something about what you do, and probably the name of your firm. That's a start. If you've answered every question and taken advantage of openings to briefly (emphasis on "briefly") tell about yourself, he or she will know what they need to know:

- Your expertise: *I handle the financial affairs for a select group of families.* The idea is not to bore HNW prospects with credentials, but rather to create interest in an area that you know relates to their present needs.

- Your attention to detail: You take the time and effort to know and understand each HNW prospect before you entertain the idea of taking them on as a client – or trying to sell them anything.

- Your abilities: You are confident enough to orchestrate this initial face time in a manner that is comfortable for everyone.

- Your image: You look and sound like a person who is comfortable around wealth, and you dress to make the right impression.

Do	Don't
Plan your first 3 minutes.	Wing it.
Smile.	Freeze your face.
Be rested.	Party the night before.
Keep your right hand free.	Make the handshake appear as a last minute thought.
Pronounce their name correctly.	Mumble their name because you can't remember how to say it right.
Prepare a self-introduction.	Expect silence to be golden – it won't be!
Dress to impress.	Dress to overpower.
Speak distinctly.	Ah….
Avoid controversy and bad mouthing.	"Did you hear about …"
Be engaging.	Bore people by talking too much.

What to Do If the Relationship Goes Quickly From *Know You* to *Conduct Business With You*

If it happens, here's what did happen. They got to know you, like you, trust you, and respect you professionally in a very short time. There are a couple of reasons why this can happen:

- There is great chemistry from the outset.
- They were introduced or referred to you by their highly trusted friend or colleague.
- They are individuals who tend to make quick decisions (see *Styles* in Chapter 7).

When and if this does happen, you need to do two things:

1. Verify that it DID happen. Test the waters by asking something like ...

    If I hear you correctly, you would like to proceed to the next step and [identify that next step]. *Are you ready to do that?*

    Their response will tell you what to do next.

2. If their response is "yes," clinch the relationship – see Chapter 10 for techniques to help you.

Helping them KNOW you is the emotional side of building rapport. Next, you will learn what to do so they will LIKE you. In the world of HNW Selling, this is a must, and chemistry has little to do with it.

7
Helping Them LIKE You

First published in 1937, Dale Carnegie's *How to Win Friends and Influence People* remains the king of the hill when it comes to people-skills books. An updated version is prominently displayed on both the Amazon and Barnes & Noble websites. Read it if you haven't already. Re-read it if you have. If you don't have time, at least implant the following points in your permanent thought process:

Dale Carnegie's Six Ways to Make People Like You

1. Become genuinely interested in other people.
2. Smile.
3. Remember that a person's name is to that person the sweetest and most important sound in any language.
4. Be a good listener. Encourage others to talk about themselves.
5. Talk in terms of the other person's interests.
6. Make the other person feel important – and do it sincerely.

Two words in the *Merriam-Webster Dictionary* definition for "like" provide helpful insight into what that word means in the context of HNW Selling: *enjoy* and *choose*. They imply a cause and effect relationship that is helpful in understanding the significance of this second step in the emotional phase of the HNW Selling decision process:

Because I *enjoy* being with you, I like you.
Because I like you, I *choose* to do business with you.

Where is this type of connection most likely to happen, on their turf or in your office? Here's a situation where a financial advisor discovered the answer the 'easy way.'

Carol made every effort to deal with clients on a professional level while also taking pains to establish personal rapport. Her office atmosphere reflected that blend. She was attracting HNW business owners, and she knew it was important to maintain that professional and personal balance.

While making a first face-to-face appointment with the owner of a flourishing biotech firm, she discovered something very important about initiating a relationship with a HNW business owner. Carol was about to say, "Why don't you come to our office …" when her prospect interrupted with, "Rather than meeting at your office, I would like to have an opportunity to show you our facilities and introduce you to some of our key people."

Carol immediately knew this was a far better way to meet for the first time. As Carol was being shown around and introduced, she was able to see their accomplishments and learn about their future plans. All Carol had to do was listen. The result: Instant rapport.

The More They Talk About Themselves, The Better They Will Like You

You may be asking, "How can I make certain my HNW prospect enjoys being with me?" As suggested by Vilfredo Pareto's principle, 20% of the time you can talk, but 80% of the time you need to listen. Which is exactly what Carnegie stressed in his last three points. I'm going to restate them in terms of what you need to do.

1. Ask questions, not about their business, but about them and their interests. If you're in their office or home, look for pictures and other items on their desk and around the room that provide clues about what is most important to them. Use the "I notice…" statement followed by a question. Example:

   I notice your son graduated from high school in June (you saw the photo). *Was that a big celebration for your family?*

2. Be a good listener. Take the *Listening Self-Inventory* quiz which follows and pay serious attention to the results.

3. When you use your 20% talk time, focus on their interests.

4. Make every sincere effort to help them feel important.

Being a good listener means truly *hearing* what they say. Many things can get in the way. Following is a self-inventory to help you separate your good listening habits from your not-so-good ones. Before you take this self-inventory, determine to be completely honest with yourself. If you really want to venture outside your comfort zone, and guarantee that you will get the most value from this inventory, have your significant other use this quiz to evaluate your listening habits. No guts, no glory!

Listening Self-Inventory

As you read through each of the following questions, circle YES or NO to indicate whether or not it represents one of your current listening habits.

1. When talking to someone, I try to pick up on other conversations around me.   YES NO

2. I sometimes pretend to pay attention when I am actually thinking about how I will respond.   YES NO

3. I frequently nod and change my facial expression to let the speaker know that he or she has my full attention.   YES NO

4. I usually respond immediately when someone has finished talking.   YES NO

5. I can usually guess what another person will say before he or she says it.   YES NO

6. I like to have people tell me only the basic facts and let me interpret the meaning for myself.   YES NO

7. I watch for any non-verbal messages (facial expressions, posture, arm and hand movements, etc.) while listening.   YES NO

8. I usually ask people to clarify what they have said rather than making any guesses about what they mean.   YES NO

See pages 102 to 103 for the lists of habits to continue and habits to eliminate.

Building Rapport with Style

Rapport means there is *harmony* in the relationship. If those we are trying to sell need and want different things than we do; if they have different ways of making decisions and solving problems; if their perceptions of people and events differ from ours; or if their efforts to communicate make us uncomfortable, achieving harmony is difficult. Difficult, but not impossible.

Differences in need, perception, and communication fall into recognizable patterns that we call *Behavioral Styles*. Much of the application of Behavioral Styles research today has its roots in the work of Dr. William Marston who defined four distinct behavioral patterns which can help us better understand the process of building rapport in a HNW Selling situation.

Much has been written about Dr. Marston's behavioral styles discovery, and many have changed the labels originally used to describe those four patterns. Thousands of consultants and trainers offer "selling with style" events and programs today. Unfortunately, I find that much of what is taught is being left back in the classroom, primarily due to a lack of emphasis on practical application. I have also found that many people would prefer to only work with clients who are more like them. My intent here is to correct both mistakes.

It's a mistake to think that you can survive in this business only working with people who are "like you." When you target HNW prospects, you soon discover they come in all shapes, sizes and styles. What will you do when you find yourself face-to-face with someone whose style is dramatically different from yours — someone with $1 million or more to invest? Style will be an issue, and you have two choices:

- Bow out.
- Learn to adapt so you can build the level of rapport required to win that person as a client.

Adapting your Behavioral Style to meet the needs of your HNW prospect's style is a vital part of helping him or her learn to like you.

It is also a mistake to think that Behavioral Styles are just great theory, but have no direct application to what you do. Glance at the four style descriptions that follow and ask yourself this question: "Do I know how to build rapport effectively with individuals in each of these styles?" If you said YES, you are a rare individual indeed. If you said NO, you're like most of us, so keep reading and you will learn how to effectively build rapport with people of all four styles.

Marston's original labels were *Controller, Emoter, Analyzer*, and *Peacemaker*. We will use labels developed by my good friend and colleague Bill Brooks as part of the *Selling Behavioral Styles* assessment tools his firm has developed. We find these tools to be outstanding, and use them in our consulting practice.

> ***Doer Style*** – These individuals seek challenge. They want to be in control, are goal oriented, and tend to make quick decisions. They want to know what your products and services can do to help them solve problems. Their decisions seem to be more rational than emotional, with a strong emphasis on their own perception of the benefits. Because of their strong ego, an important emotional dimension is involved in each decision they make. Words and phrases used to describe them …

- Direct, dominating, take charge.
- Competitive and naturally aggressive.
- Quick, impulsive, always pressed for time, impatient.
- Outspoken.
- Under pressure – they can be belligerent.
- Their greatest fear – someone will take unfair advantage of them.

Famous Doers …

~ Henry Ford I
~ Malcolm X
~ Christopher Columbus
~ Margaret Thatcher
~ Ghenghis Khan
~ Ross Perot
~ George W. Bush

Talker Style – These individuals are engaging, creative, and entertaining. They thrive on influencing others, and they love socializing. They're unpredictable and seem to take their time reaching a decision. That's because they are sizing you up. Then suddenly they decide, basically because they feel they want to do business with you. To them, YOU are your products and services. Their decision-making is strongly emotional, but you'll also discover a rational side that is based primarily on their judgments concerning you. Words and phrases used to describe them include …

- Outgoing, people oriented, very friendly.
- Enthusiastic, popular, easy to talk with.
- Charming and eloquent.
- Stylish and trendy.
- Positive and optimistic
- Under pressure – they can become very emotional and overbearing.
- Their greatest fear – that they will become overbearing and cause conflict.

Famous Talkers …

~ Beethoven
~ Winston Churchill
~ Muhammad Ali
~ Ronald Reagan
~ Pablo Picasso
~ William Clinton

Pacer Style – These individuals like everything planned in advance, and they appreciate the personal touch. They want things to be non-threatening and friendly. They can make decisions fairly quickly, and those decisions are a more balanced blend of emotion and rationalization. They will want to know how your products and services will meet their needs. Words and phrases used to describe them include …

- Easygoing, steady, process oriented, slower paced.
- Predictable, consistent.
- Accepts others slowly, prefers routine work flow.
- Accommodating, willing, conforming.
- Under pressure – they tend to slow down and back off.
- Their greatest fear – unplanned change.

Famous Pacers …

~ Gerald Ford
~ Helen Keller
~ Dwight Eisenhower
~ Robert E. Lee
~ Albert Gore
~ George Bush Sr.

Controller Style – These individuals want facts and information presented in a logical manner, and they want everything documented. They thrive on details, and are perfectionists who want things well organized and predictable. They do not appreciate the "personal touch." Their decisions are more rational, but emotionally so. In other words, there is strong emotion behind their rationalizations. They will want to know how your products and services can solve problems, and they will want proof. Words and phrases used to describe them include …

• Cool, distant, reserved, diplomatic, courteous, restrained.
• They think things through before acting.
• Concerned about accuracy, precision, and making everything comply to their standards.
• Prefer data, facts, and order.
• Objective, conservative, closed-minded, and unemotional (until they are challenged).
• Under pressure – they tend to become critical and fearful.
• Their greatest fear – that they will make mistakes and be criticized.

Famous Controllers...

~ Michelangelo
~ Albert Einstein
~ Woodrow Wilson
~ Eleanor Roosevelt
~ Thomas Jefferson
~ Jimmy Carter

Building rapport involves establishing harmonious relationships with people whose Behavioral Styles may be very different from our own. The above style descriptions give you a flavor of this challenging task. To demonstrate rapport building, imagine that in your first face-to-face meeting, you sense that the HNW prospect sitting across from you is very different from you. Here's what you can do.

Step 1: Read the other person's Behavioral Style ...

- You can make an **initial reading in about 60 seconds**. As you observe the other person, ask "Is this person outgoing and active, or more reserved?"

> Outgoing and Active – they are either a ...
>
> ◊ DOER – if they are direct, outspoken, competitive, and impatient.
> ◊ TALKER – if they are talkative, enthusiastic, charming, optimistic, and stylish.

> Reserved – they are either a ...
>
> ◊ PACER – if they are easygoing, slower paced, warm, and friendly.
> ◊ CONTROLLER – if they are distant, reserved, courteous, restrained, and unemotional.

- Next, look for CLUES that either confirm or contradict your initial reading.

DOER

Fast paced speech
Comes on strong
Tries to control the situation
Watches the time

TALKER

Friendly and talkative
Uses many hand gestures
Shows much emotion
Doesn't watch the time

PACER

Easygoing
Unemotional voice
Deliberate and methodical
Patient

CONTROLLER

Speaks slowly
Asks questions about facts
Deliberates
Uses few gestures

Step 2: Be clear about your own Behavioral Style and recognize potential Compatibility Issues.

• Your Behavioral Style is _____.

> We have a Behavioral Style Assessment Tool and Profile to help you define and gain valuable insights into your style. For more information, call us toll free: 800-883-6582

• If you discover **your style is the same as your prospect's**, be aware that like styles tend to be compatible socially. This should help your HNW prospect enjoy being with you and to ultimately choose to do business with you. However, conflict can occur when like styles work together.

• **Mixed styles** tend to be more compatible when working together, but less in social situations. Take note of these combinations ...

MOST Compatible ...

◊ Socially – Pacer and Controller
◊ Working Together – Doer and Pacer, Talker and Pacer,
   Controller and Pacer

LEAST Compatible ...

◊ Socially – Doer and Controller
◊ Working Together – Doer and Talker, Doer and Controller

Step 3: Understand that harmony does <u>not</u> depend on compatibility.
Harmony results from awareness, flexibility, and adaptability.

- **Awareness** – Results from everything you have read thus far. You
  are aware of each Behavioral Styles' characteristics. You are aware
  of your Style and the Style of the person sitting across from you.
  You are aware of the compatibility issues that may exist.

- **Flexibility** – Is primarily an attitude. When you discover potential
  compatibility issues between you and your prospect, you must be
  flexibile (attitude) in order to become *adaptable* (behavior).

- **Adaptability** – Is the behavioral shift necessary to achieve harmony.

Step 4: Adapt your style to the needs of the other person in order to
create harmony and build rapport. In the 1970s, Richard Bandler and
John Grinder began to shift their psychotherapy studies into an area now
known as Neuro-Linguistic Programming, or NLP. They discovered that
the key to building rapport is the ability to step into the other person's
world by assuming a similar state of mind.

Once this mental shift occurs, you focus on aligning your body language
to match and model the other person's natural behaviors. It works
because everyone's physical state is closely tied to his or her emotional
state. This is the basis for what we call *Adaptability*.

The necessity to adapt your Behavioral Style to meet the needs of the other person continues throughout the HNW Selling process. We will provide tips on how to make those adjustments throughout the book, but for now, we'll focus strictly on the **LIKE You** phase.

Following are ways to adapt your style to build rapport with each of the styles.

Adapting to the DOER Style

- Suggest a time frame. If they agree, stick to it.
- Sit erect and be attentive.
- Smile, but don't use a lot of gestures and emotion.
- Avoid small talk – talk only about what's relevant to them.
- Don't go into details unless asked.
- As the conversation leads to their finances, focus on end results.

Adapting to the TALKER Style

- Don't worry about time. They'll take whatever time they want.
- Sit up, but be relaxed and expressive.
- Smile, laugh, and use many hand gestures while speaking.
- Don't worry about small talk, simply let them go where they want to go.
- Give limited details, unless asked. You probably won't be.
- As the conversation leads to their finances, tell stories and provide testimonies of experts.

Adapting to the PACER Style

- Suggest a time frame. Confirm the ending time about 10 minutes before the deadline.
- Sit erect, but be relaxed and pleasant.
- Keep body language controlled. Use some gestures, but don't overdo it.
- Listen patiently and speak with a sincere tone of voice.
- Some details are OK, but present them in a logical order.
- As the conversation leads to their finances, present a planned approach, but don't be overly expressive or optimistic.

Adapting to the CONTROLLER Style

- Ask about their time frame. When they give it, stick with it.
- Sit erect, and be very attentive.
- Restrain body language.
- Control emotions. Slow down and listen. When you speak, be very sincere.
- Provide full details, with evidence.
- As the conversation leads to their finances, present details with all the evidence you can to back up what you say.

Developing the HABITS of Good Listening

(Reference – *Listening Self-Inventory*, page 93.)

Normally people think about four times as fast as the average rate of speech, which is 125 words per minute. It's only natural to let our minds wander, to listen for facts and skip over the details, or begin to think about how to respond. Consequently, it is estimated that the average person listens with about 25% efficiency.

The Habits to CONTINUE on the Inventory are 3, 6, 7, and 8. You might want to review them once again.

The Habits to ELIMINATE are 1, 2, 4, and 5 – for the following reasons.

- Eliminate Habit #1 – Attention is a critical element of effective communication. Concentration is enhanced by maintaining good eye contact, nodding affirmatively, and responding audibly with a genuine, "Oh, is that right?" or some similar phrase. If it will help, ask yourself a question and listen for the answer as the other person speaks.

- Eliminate Habit #2 – If you begin to think of your response before the other person finishes speaking, you will miss important details. You need to concentrate. Remind yourself of that with each exchange. Take notes if appropriate.

- Eliminate Habit #4 – When you do concentrate and listen effectively, you need to collect your thoughts before responding. You may also want to hear more. Pause before responding — take a full breath and count to three. (Note the relationship between habits 2 and 4!)

- Eliminate Habit #5 – Making assumptions about what people are about to say causes people to interrupt before the other person is finished. That says, "I am not listening and do not care what you have to say." Make certain they finish speaking before you respond. This will ensure that you "got it."

What They Need to Like about You

They know you. That's already happened. What you hope will happen after they leave your meeting is that they will say to someone, "What I like about him/her is…" If you've asked key questions, listened to hear what they say, talked mostly about what interests them, and created rapport, they will like you because you accomplished the following.

- Connected with their interests, and encouraged them to talk about things important to them.
- Avoided forcing your agenda on them.
- Made them feel important, and did it sincerely.
- Recognized any differences between their Behavioral Style and yours, and took appropriate steps to adapt your style to their needs.

To make certain you do that, here's a list of do's and don'ts from this chapter to keep key points fresh in your memory:

Do	Don't
Assess your own Behavioral Style.	Assume they'll be like you.
Smile.	Think only about what you're going to say. Forget to smile.
Ask questions about their interests.	Ask something like, "Did I tell you about…?"
Be sincere.	Simply try to look sincere.
Assess and confirm their Behavioral Style.	Guess and don't bother to look for confirming clues.

Do	Don't
Have a flexible attitude.	Think you're too good a financial advisor for this.
Adapt your style to match and model theirs.	Try and be manipulative.

Knowing you and even liking you does not necessarily mean they trust you. You need to earn that trust, and there are specific ways to do that. You will learn how in Chapter 8.

8

Getting Them to TRUST You

Frequently television and print ads use a mountain climbing theme, suggesting you have reached the peak when you buy their product. It's a great image. It is also an accurate way to understand the significance that *trust* plays in helping a HNW prospect finalize a relationship with you as their "go-to" financial quarterback. Scaling a mountain takes time and hard work, and you need to be careful not to slip and slide your way back down to the bottom.

Trust is visceral. *I trust you* means that I am relying on your intent and ability to deliver whatever will meet my needs in the future — tomorrow, next week, next year. For trust to happen, there must to be something happening now that provides evidence and assurance that my trust will not be in vain.

As our research solidly demonstrates, people with serious money do not want a salesperson advising them on how to protect and grow their money. Traditional sales tactics do not mix well with trust-building. If you come across as "salesy" in your efforts to convince a HNW prospect to like you, your efforts could be undermined by the "But can I really trust you?" question. The longer that question remains, the more difficult it will be to overcome.

Your objective is to identify and eliminate any of the built-in resistance HNW prospects typically have toward salespeople in general.

> **Avoid the temptation to hand them your brochure or collateral materials at this stage.**

That is what they expect a salesperson to do, and it is an automatic trigger for that "Can I trust you?" question.

> **Don't attempt to be too friendly, too knowledgeable, or too anything.**

You will come across as someone trying too hard to sell and will trigger those defense mechanisms HNW people use to protect themselves.

There's that paradox again! You ultimately have to sell your services, but the effort must be so refined, so well-honed, that it becomes seamless. Seamless selling skills will make your Critical Path journey profitable. Everything you do along the way is significant, but building trust may be the most important. Trust is the foundation of everything else you do.

Trust is dynamically intertwined with two other concepts: *credibility* and *integrity*. It is YOU that clients either do or do not trust; not your company or the products and services you provide. Credibility, that quality of being believable and trustworthy, is a human quality. So is integrity, which you can only maintain by adhering to the moral principles that guide your profession.

> **When your prospect sees ongoing evidence of credibility and integrity, he or she will trust you.**

Trust is not the hype of motivational talks and pithy sayings. It is clearly defined, real, well documented, and vital to bringing the emotional and rational dimensions of the buying decision into sync.

Little Things Mean a Lot

In *Cultivating the Affluent II: Leveraging High-Net Worth Client and Advisor Relationships*, Russ Alan Prince and Karen Maru point out that many more HNW clients leave their financial advisors when a failure in the relationship reduces their level of trust rather than because of poor portfolio performance. It's true, some HNW investors do focus on short-term performance, but most are looking for continual evidence of credibility and integrity.

> *I was meeting with the leader of a wealth management team that has been successful in all areas: retaining and upgrading present HNW clients plus bringing in new ones. As we were talking, his junior partner stuck his head into the conference room and apologized for not being able to sit in on our meeting because, as he put it, "We have a good client who is in the process of trans-*

ferring in another 10 million dollars, and I need to be certain everything is flawless."

As he darted out the door, his senior partner smiled and commented, "Like every other advisor, our investments are down, but we deliver first class service and are aggressive in managing all aspects of each client's every expectation." He went on to explain that their mantra is to be the "Trusted Advisor" — to always do first class business in a first class manner. As he talked, it was clear they did the little things very well.

When you consider the critical role that credibility and integrity play in your relationships with HNW prospects and clients, it's important to recognize that evidence of your credibility and integrity begins with your first face-to-face encounter.

Were you on time? Did you ...

- Handle those first three minutes as planned?
- Pronounce their name correctly and introduce yourself smoothly?
- Project the right image?
- Speak clearly and distinctly?
- Avoid controversy and bad mouthing?
- Avoid talking too much?

As the meeting unfolded, did you ...

- Connect with them and get them talking about their interests?
- Make them feel important, and do it sincerely?
- Watch for clues about their Behavioral Style and then take appropriate steps to adapt your style to their needs?
- Focus on solutions and processes, not products?

These are some of the little things that mean a lot. For every honest "yes" you answered to these questions, the better you did to establish credibility from the outset. You will continue to build credibility and integrity by doing the following without exception.

To build credibility:

- Continue to be on time, every time.

- Promptly return phone calls.

- Respond to every phone call, e-mail, and fax within the designated time frame, or within 24 hours maximum.

- Never say, "Trust me." Instead, state what you will do, and then do it.

- Admit when you don't know the answer, promise to find the answer, and then follow through.

To establish integrity:

- Answer questions specifically rather than evasively.

- Don't do things you said you wouldn't do.

- Don't lie about anything.

- Don't mislead.

- Maintain eye contact.

The Big Things That Matter

When we conducted our initial research on how affluent investors rated their financial advisors, we expected to find that all was not well. However, we were surprised to discover the extent of the dissatisfaction. Nine of the twelve areas we measured showed statistically significant gaps between what affluent investors expected and the actual performance of their advisors.

That initial study was in early 1999 — a great time for investors. Studies in 2002 and 2003 show that dissatisfaction among HNW investors continues to grow. In Chapter 1, we listed the top three complaints: not receiving satisfactory value, not trusting the quality of advice, and not trusting that the advice given is always in their best interest. Notice the clear interplay between *trust* and *value*.

Little things will help to build trust, but as prospective HNW clients consider trusting your advice for the management of their considerable assets, value begins to loom larger and larger in their minds. There is more to it than dollars. Value will be measured by what you specifically do to shape your relationship with them. Actually, this is very good news for you.

As you read through the following list, think of ways you can maintain what you now provide while continually adding value in the months to come. Added value builds deeper trust, which is the most effective strategy you can have for building competitive advantage. Here are eight factors you can use to measure the value you provide to your clients.

1. **Protection** – You are helping clients set financial goals, determine a portfolio asset allocation strategy, and select investments and financial products that will enable them to achieve their goals and continually protect their assets.

2. **Selection** – Your clients have an opportunity to select from the best investments and financial products available, and your advice helps them select wisely.

3. **Information** – Your clients have easy access to portfolio and other key information that is presented in language they can understand.

4. **Service Quality** – The service your clients receive is characterized by speed, accuracy, responsiveness, error correction, and all those "little" things performed at or beyond their expectation.

5. **Convenience** – Service location, hours, and delivery are where and when clients need and want it.

6. **Personal Attention** – Frequent and timely contact with each client is maintained by you and other key people. Your attention is proactive, not reactive.

7. **Emotional Satisfaction** – Simplicity, a sense of belonging, familiarity, recognition, and an inviting office environment all work together to create a sense of prestige and satisfaction.

8. **Financial Impact** – Reasonable fees, tax savings, adequate protection, and acceptable growth all work together to provide each client with a desired return on investment.

If you can deliver these value factors, you will far exceed HNW investor expectations in all twelve areas of dissatisfaction uncovered by our initial research – plus any other concerns revealed since then. This is a goal worth pursuing, and one well within your reach.

What They Need to Trust You

Knowing you and liking you is not enough. When asked why they stay with you, you want your HNW clients to say, "Because I trust him!" or "Because I trust her!" When they do say that, it will be because you did the following.

- Always placed the prospect's best interests first.
- Continue to be on time with everything from phone calls to meetings.
- Responded promptly to any effort to communicate with you.
- Stated what you will do instead of simply saying, "Trust me."
- Promised to find answers you didn't know, and then did so.
- Answered questions clearly and specifically.
- Did not do what you said you would not do.
- Never lied or misled.
- Looked them in the eye.
- Continually added meaningful value to as many aspects of the relationship as possible.

Although this list may not be complete, the principle is clear. You earn the trust of HNW people.

Here is a list of do's and don'ts to keep key points from this chapter fresh in your memory:

Do	Don't
Enter appointments in your day timer immediately when you make them.	Write appointments on a slip of paper to be entered later.
Look forward to talking with them.	Think, "I'll call them later."
Clearly and specifically explain what you will do.	Say, "Trust me, I'll take care of it."

Do	Don't
View questions as an opportunity to maintain contact.	Think, "What can I say to get them off my back?"
Call them first if you find you must do what you said you wouldn't.	Think, "They'll never find out."
Say, "That's something I can't discuss" rather than lie.	Talk about something you shouldn't.
Maintain frequent eye contact.	Keep looking down or at the clock to avoid eye contact.
Use the eight value factors as a checklist – and continually seek ways to add value to each client relationship.	Look at something (anything!) on the value factors list and say, "I can't do that."
Create the impression of a professional, eager to help.	Be too talkative, pushy, or "salesy."

There's a very simple principle involved here. If HNW prospects learn to trust you, they will find a way to enter into a business relationship with you.

Selling HNW Prospects

Chapter 9
Earning Their RESPECT

Chapter 10
Clinching the Relationship

9

Earning Their RESPECT

You are *trusted* for what you are expected to do, but you are *respected* for what you are doing now. **Professional respect is directly related to the manner in which you deliver your services**. As you demonstrate your expertise to a HNW prospect from the moment they start getting to know you, their professional respect for you builds.

In Chapter 8, we emphasized how trust is vital to bringing the emotional and rational dimensions of the buying decision together. But long before trust is established, your HNW prospect will begin to move beyond the intuitive emotional aspect of their decision-making and look at things more rationally. Sounds logical, but what does it mean?

Setting Emotions Aside, But Not Totally

We make rational decisions as we evaluate alternatives and make choices we believe are consistent with our values and expectations. We can be deliberate and rational in our evaluations, but we can also be very emphatic about our values and preferences. Our emotions are never totally set aside.

One of the contributing factors in helping your HNW prospect LIKE you is your ability to adapt to the needs of their Behavioral Style. As they move into the more rational dimension of their decision to use your services, it will be helpful to focus on how each Behavior Style rationalizes decisions.

- *Doer Style* – Because they like to take charge and find challenges in new opportunities, they will tend to rationalize the benefits each alternative will provide. They will want to know how you provide those benefits and the probability of success. Once they see those benefits clearly, they typically make quick decisions.

- *Talker Style* – Because they are highly people oriented and work hard to influence others, they will rationalize your ability to deliver

— along with their ability to influence you toward meeting their needs. They also want a friendly relationship because they detest interpersonal conflict. Once they feel good about the relationship, they can make a quick decision.

- *Pacer Style* – Because they like everything planned in advance, they will pay close attention to the steps in your Financial Advisory Process. Once they are convinced the process is logical and rational, and you are consistent and trustworthy, they will finally decide.

- *Controller Style* – Because they are perfectionists who thrive on organization and details, they will evaluate and rationalize everything. Like the Doers, they will look at the solutions you provide, and they will be particularly concerned about proof. They may even want proof of your proof. They are much slower and deliberate in making decisions than any of the other styles.

They Care About Solutions, Not Services

You will be tempted to tell each new HNW prospect about your services at every opportunity, but you need to resist the temptation.

You earn professional respect through *demonstrating* your expertise.

Expertise goes beyond what you know. It's your skill in applying your knowledge to specific situations that matter. HNW prospects are looking for solutions.

Earlier, you helped them LIKE you by asking questions to get them talking about themselves. Now you need to continue asking questions, but for a different purpose. You will ask probing questions to uncover needs, values, and expectations.

But before you begin to ask probing questions, ask permission to ask – then ask permission to take notes. It goes something like this:

It would be helpful if I could learn more about _____ (see A next page). *Do you mind if I ask a few questions?*

Is it all right if I take some notes? (see B below)

A – If you discover they are facing a significant Financial Impact Point, make that the focus of your inquiry. Examples are selling a business, receiving a large inheritance, or deciding to exercise a significant stock option. Otherwise, you can simply say *"...about your financial situation."*

B – You take notes for two reasons. First, and most important, to help you concentrate and avoid forgetting their answers later. Second, to show your prospect that this is no idle chatter. The "serious stuff" has started.

The questions you ask should help you define their needs and clarify the values and expectations that will influence their decisions. Here are some tips to help you formulate your questions:

1. When **probing to uncover their needs**, use specific what, who, where, when, how, and why questions that will provide the information you need, and demonstrate your knowledge and skill. For example, if you want to probe the upcoming sale of their business, you might ask such things as …

    *   *Why have you decided to sell your business at this time?*
    *   *Who is buying your business, and what is their relationship to you?*
    *   *How did you decide they were the right buyers?*
    *   *What knowledge and skills do buyers have that will enable them to continue running the business?*
    *   *How will the buyers finance the purchase? How is payment guaranteed?*
    *   *Why did you decide to accept that type of buy-out arrangement?*
    *   *Have you prepared an operating statement and valuation report?*
    *   *What are your plans after leaving the business?*

    Through these questions, and those you continue to ask as they respond, you will demonstrate your expertise and begin earning their professional respect.

To make certain you're prepared, take each of the following *Financial Impact Points* and formulate a series of questions to help you cover all the potential financial and personal needs that could emerge.

• Selling their business or professional practice.

• Exercising stock options.

• Signing a massive contract (massive in financial terms).

• Selling a large capital asset.

• Taking a new job with a new, large compensation package – in the same company or elsewhere.

• Getting ready to retire.

• Receiving an inheritance.

• Facing divorce – both those who control the assets and those who will have to negotiate to receive a portion of those assets.

There are also *Areas of Dissatisfaction* you should be prepared to probe:

• A financial problem they don't know how to address.

• The possibility of a contentious divorce.

• Dissatisfaction with their current broker, advisor, insurance agent, financial planner, banker, etc.

• Frustration with current market fluctuations.

2. You should also insert questions at appropriate points that **uncover their values and expectations**. Here are a few examples that you might use when asking about the pending sale of a business:

• *Why is it important to have your oldest son take over your business?*

• *Why is it important to sell the business now instead of when you are closer to age 65?*

• *What do you expect will happen to the company's profit picture over the next 2 or 3 years with this leveraged buyout arrangement?*

• *What tax implications do you expect from this arrangement?*

3. As you begin to uncover needs, values, and expectations, you can further demonstrate your expertise by **presenting alternative solutions** and asking which they prefer. Here's an example:

> *You've been trying to decide how to structure the purchase of your business by your son. We've talked about an installment purchase and a private annuity. Which do you think you would prefer at this point?*

(After they respond)

> *Which do you think would be your son's choice?*

If you have not uncovered a *Financial Impact Point* or *Area of Dissatisfaction*, you can still ask questions to probe and define their needs. You can also clarify the values and expectations that will influence their decisions. Again, it's important to formulate basic questions you can use in these situations. Here is a list to explore with them. Each area is described in lay rather than technical terms. For example, "Insuring against serious financial loss due to medical bills and not being able to work" rather than "medical and disability insurance." Use the same type of everyday language to formulate your questions.

Financial Obligations

- Meeting current financial obligations.
- Reducing or eliminating debt.

Lifestyle

- Maintaining or upgrading current lifestyle.
- Providing for future financial security.

Budget, Net Worth, and Emergency Planning

- Documenting current net worth.
- Budgeting revenue and expenses.
- Determining how many months' income to set aside for emergencies.

Insurance

- Insuring against serious financial loss due to medical bills and not being able to work.
- Insuring against serious financial loss from having to replace or

repair damage to their home, vehicles, and other real estate and property.

• Using insurance for wealth transfer, tax management, wealth preservation, inheritance planning, and wealth accumulation.

Long-Term Care

• Determining potential long-term care needs.

• Purchasing LTC insurance or planning to self-insure.

Education

• Paying for their children's present private school education.

• Paying for their own or their spouse's degree completion.

• Supporting their children's post high-school education.

• Supporting educational efforts of other family members or friends.

Investments

• Assessing risk tolerance and establishing an investment policy.

• Establishing investment goals.

• Managing asset allocation in relation to investment goals.

• Examining performance in relation to investment goals.

• Revising individual investments as appropriate.

Taxes

• Minimizing the amount of tax paid to federal, state, and local governments.

Giving

• Establishing a charitable giving plan that is consistent with their values and compatible with the rest of their financial needs, goals, and priorities.

Retirement

• Determining their desired retirement age.

• Determining their desired income level at retirement.

• Determining their desired lifestyle in retirement.

Estate Planning

- Having a detailed plan of how and to whom property, valuables, and money will be distributed upon death.

- Determining family values; relationships with children (if grown) and their families (in-laws, grandchildren, etc.), special circumstances, extended family members, charitable causes, etc.

They're Looking for Evidence That Shows You Can Deliver

If you ask the right questions, what they need and want will become clear to you. Their professional respect for you will grow in the process, and they will be ready to hear you say something like ...

I (we) have considerable experience working with situations like yours. This is an area of specialty for us.

After the questions you ask and the information they provide, they should not be surprised to hear that kind of statement. However, saying that you can deliver is not enough — they will be looking for evidence.

The best way to provide that **evidence** is by explaining how you have provided solutions in similar situations. For your story to be credible and have the impact you want, it must include the following:

- **Confidentiality** – Neither the situation nor the people involved should be identified, and the prospect should not be able to guess who it is.

- **Familiar situation** — If this prospect is selling their business, use another business sale situation. They must be able to identify with the situation you describe, and the specific solution you provided must be familiar.

- **Similar solution** – It does not have to be exactly the same, but similar financial components need to be there. If you're focusing on a tax relief solution, the financing of the sale could be different, but a tax issue must be included.

- **Desired consequences** – This is the real evidence. You need to explain how the outcome of applying this solution provided anticipated and favorable consequences.

It would be beneficial for you to document and prepare to use as many of these stories as possible. Write up those stories, store them, and include them at every opportunity.

Sell What You Will Deliver

Guess what?! Even though you ask great questions, tell them you have considerable experience working with situations like theirs, and provide the evidence to support that claim, your prospect wants to know one more thing. HOW do you work with a client to achieve what you have described? What process do you use? How will you work with them if they become your client?

If you clinch this relationship, the solutions you provide will be delivered incrementally over the months and, hopefully, years to come. Remember, a failed relationship (not poor portfolio performance) is the main reason affluent clients leave their financial advisors (Prince & Maru, Chapter 6). Your **Financial Advisory Process** is an intangible, but you have already provided tangible evidence that your process works.

So now is the time to test the waters to see if your HNW prospect is open to learning more about how you work with clients. Immediately after you tell your story of evidence, it's a great time to say ...

> *We maintain a close working relationship with a select group of families. If it's OK, I'd like to take a few minutes to show you how we work with our clients. Is that agreeable with you?*

You'll likely get a "Sure, I'd like to see that" response. They will probably wonder how they can be certain you will be around enough to provide those kinds of solutions. Here are three ways to do respond.

1. Reach into your briefcase and take out a copy of your **Promotional Piece** (brochure). Open it up, and use it as a visual aid while you describe your Financial Advisory Process and explain how each step

will benefit them. Here is how that Promotional Piece should be organized.

- **Value Commitment** – On the cover should be a statement describing the value you bring to a client relationship. For example ...

[Company name] serves as a solutions provider for all aspects of our clients' finances. We provide a unique combination of *capital preservation* and *wealth creation strategies.*

By working with a select group of individuals and businesses, we ensure thorough attention to each of our clients' specific needs. With our carefully orchestrated Financial Advisory Process, we assure you that all financial decisions we make on your behalf will be consistent with your goals.

- **Our Financial Practice Team** – Photos and a brief bio on each.

- **Financial Advisory Process** – An overview of your process with a list of the steps involved. Follow that with a separate page for each step. On each of those pages, describe the step — and state the specific benefits the client will receive.

Give them a copy of your *Promotional Piece* as a tangible reminder of all the details you have been discussing. A simple glance at the cover later will remind them of the key things that initially caught their attention.

Whether you use a *Promotional Piece* as I described or a brochure you've had for a while, neither will earn you professional respect with a HNW prospect. At best, a well conceived piece of collateral material can communicate structure and clarity about who you are, what you do, how you do it, and the benefits of working with you. Remember, however, a slick brochure reeks "sales piece."

You are the product! Who you are, how you conduct yourself, and the seamless professionalism of your HNW Selling process are all factors that will ultimately influence a HNW prospect's decision to conduct business with you. Do not let your ego become all wrapped up in a fancy brochure.

"Could you take a look at my new brochure?" asked a financial advisor following a talk I delivered for his firm. As I perused this beautiful piece, I noted that it resembled a four color annual report from a Fortune 500 company, except his picture appeared throughout. He went on to explain that one of his clients owned an advertising agency and was the creator. Of course the brochure was a deal, costing only $8,000 when the going rate was supposedly twice that amount.

After thumbing through his brochure, I looked up, suggested that I was an ideal prospect for him, and asked "Why should I do business with you?" His only response was, "Read the brochure."

His mouth opened as I began tearing his brochure in half. I said, "If you can't effectively and smoothly answer why I should do business with you, no $8,000 brochure is going to do it for you." Although I was being a bit rough on him, he got the point.

2. Show your HNW prospect a sample of the ***Financial Organizer*** they will receive when they become your client. This loose-leaf organizer provides a convenient way to store all the documentation relating to the process you will use and the solutions you will provide. Your sample should include the following.

    - Tab 1 – A description of your Financial Advisory Process
    - Tab 2 – Their Financial Plan (They will see that once you have gathered all their financial information together, this will be the next step.)
    - Tab 3 – Ongoing Review (It lists the Milestone Meetings you will have with them plus the written reports of those meetings.)
    - Tab 4 – Budgeting & Cash Flow Management
    - Tab 5 – Net Worth Statement
    - Tab 6 – Insurance
    - Tab 7 – Investments
    - Tab 8 – Education Plan

- Tab 9 – Tax Information
- Tab 10 – Retirement Plan
- Tab 11 – Estate Plan
- Tab 12 – Charitable Giving Plan

Remember Jay?   He's the former transactional broker turned HNW financial quarterback in Chapter 1. The reason Jay has been able to continue along his Critical Path and grow his business without a brochure is because he carries a *Financial Organizer* with him everywhere he goes.

> *"It's a flat-out magnet for assets," responded Jay, when I asked how he used the organizer. "I can see the prospect's eyes open as I remove it from my briefcase. Sooner or later the prospect will say something like, 'My financial advisor doesn't do anything like this.' Then I know I've got them,"*
> *Jay explained.*

> *Without realizing it, Jay was using his Financial Organizer to differentiate himself from the competition. He found it to be so powerful that it became his constant sales piece. Keep in mind, Jay is a true master at HNW Selling and has rehearsed every move. Without that skill, the Financial Organizer would be a showpiece instead of a solution.*

3.   Skillfully use a bit of **reverse psychology** to communicate the win-win type of relationship you will provide.   Assuming you have now established rapport and a suitable level of trust, you want your HNW prospect to seriously think, "This is the type of go-to financial advisor I'm looking for." Tell them …

> *Our approach begins with profiling every prospective client so we can determine the answers to two questions. First, can we truly provide the solutions you seek and help you with all your financial needs? Second, is this a good fit – is there sufficient rapport and trust so we can work effectively with you? There is also another good reason. You need to profile us, to look under our hood and ask yourself those same two questions. Our experience clearly tells us this must be a mutually beneficial situation for it to work.*

I do want to caution you about using reverse psychology. You must use it honestly and sincerely, or you will come across as arrogant and be perceived as simply another manipulative salesperson — the last message you want to communicate at this point (or any point)!

Your Financial Advisory Process is the product you will deliver, and that is what you should ultimately sell. Everything to this point has been in preparation for this sales presentation. As you use your Promotional Piece to help you explain your **Financial Advisory Process,** and show them a sample of the *Financial Organizer* as tangible evidence of what they will receive, you can continually make reference back to the questions you have asked and the issues that those questions raised.

Jack was a stockbroker who, like many brokers, finally decided he was better suited to be a go-to financial quarterback than an investment advisor. Taking his top 15 clients through his new Financial Advisory Process one-at-a-time, he was able to convert each to a fee-based arrangement. The promise of a personalized Financial Organizer was a powerful tool. In the process, he raised an additional five million dollars. Even more significant, eight of these top clients informed him that they had been actively seeking another advisor.

They trusted Jack as a person, but they no longer wanted a stockbroker. When Jack used his newly acquired HNW Selling skills to present the new and improved version of his professional self, his existing HNW clients opted to stay with him.

Managing Expectations

How would you handle an ideal HNW prospect — someone you have been romancing for a long time— who finally decides to give you their serious money, but demands an unrealistic return? The following occurred in February 2000, before the market dropped.

"I'm going to give you all of my 40 million dollars from the sale of my business, but I want a 20% return," demanded the HNW prospect.

"Oh," replied the financial advisor very calmly, "so what you're telling me is you want to take a lot of risk with your 40 million dollars. Is that right?"

"No," answered the HNW prospect, "I just want to get a 20% return."

"That's understandable, but it means you definitely will be taking considerable risk with your 40 million dollars. There is no other way to achieve that level of return," explained the financial advisor. "Anyone who says different is not being honest with you."

From that point forward, the financial advisor was in complete control of their working relationship. Not only did he clinch the deal with a HNW prospect he had been pursuing for months, **he began managing the client's expectations from the outset.**

How much professional respect do you think that honesty earned the financial advisor in the eyes of his new HNW client? It was enough to gain an introduction to three of his new client's HNW friends, within the next thirty days.

What They Need to Respect You Professionally

When they know you, like you, and trust you will deliver, you have accomplished a lot! But before you can clinch the relationship, you must gain their professional respect. You want them to be thinking, "I'm convinced!" When they actually do say "I am ready," it will be because you did the following:

- Continued to adapt to their Behavioral Style, and recognized that the rational dimension of their decision to use your services is also important.

- Used probing questions to uncover their needs, values, and expectations.

- Stated clearly that you had considerable experience in working with situations similar to the one they were experiencing.

- Used stories to provide evidence that you could deliver.

- Received their permission to use your *Promotional Piece* to show them how you would work with them – and how that would benefit them.

- Showed them your *Financial Organizer* and gave them your *Promotional Piece* to provide tangible evidence of your intangible advisory process.

- Carefully and skillfully applied reverse psychology to clarify how each of you need to evaluate the potential of establishing a working relationship.

- Managed any unrealistic expectations, so those expectations would not come back later to haunt you.

To make certain you earn their respect and manage their expectations, here's a list of do's and don'ts from this chapter to keep key points fresh in your memory:

Do	Don't
Continue looking for clues so you can effectively adapt to their Behavioral Style as they move into the more rational dimension.	Assume you've already "connected" with them and no further adapting will be needed.
Ask permission to probe deeper – and take notes.	Simply jump in and start asking probing questions that could alarm them.
Prepare questions in advance for key Financial Impact Points and potential Areas of Dissatisfaction.	Wing it, thinking "I'm pretty good at this."
Ask – take notes – and keep asking until you have a good overview of their situation.	Ask a few questions and think "I'm glad that's over – now I can start selling."
Start building a bridge toward clinching the relationship with a "considerable experience in that area" statement.	Start telling stories without first giving your "considerable experience" reason for doing so.

Do	Don't
Use a story of evidence only if you have one you can legitimately share.	Make up a story on the spot and risk damaging your credibility.
Use your Promotional Piece to discuss your Financial Advisory Process.	Use your Promotional Piece to broadly describe your services or simply to impress them.
Keep the entire focus on them and their needs.	Start talking about yourself, especially when "story time" comes.
Profile and communicate that you are selective.	Come across as too anxious or manipulative.
Establish and manage expectations.	Allow clients to be unrealistic.
Carry a Financial Organizer with you at all times to provide tangible evidence of your value.	Find yourself saying, "If I had a Financial Organizer with me, I could show you."

10

Clinching the Relationship

Yes Martha, you do have to close that sale! We call it "clinching the relationship," because that more accurately describes what needs to happen in your situation. *Closing* is a transactional sales term, but your goal is to establish a long-term HNW client relationship.

That does not, however, change the fact — a *sales close* is required. Why devote an entire chapter to it? Because studies continually show that the vast majority of people who sell don't close simply because they don't ask. Some studies say 50 percent fail to ask; others suggest as high as 62 percent. Another 35 percent will ask for the order, accept whatever excuse is given for not buying at that time, and never ask again.

There was a great article in the June 18, 2002, Greensboro *News & Record* that every parent can appreciate, and it does have some relevance here. A May 2002 study confirmed what you and I have always known about kids: if they ask enough times, kids usually get what they want. Focusing on ages 12-17, the study found that nine is the average number of times kids have to ask their parents before they finally give in. If that's all it takes, there's no reason you can't close every sale.

Obviously, nagging is not what you need to do. But you do need to ask, and in many cases more than once.

Be Prepared For a Sequence of Mini-Closes

Going back to your prospecting efforts in Chapter 3, there is actually a sequence of closes you need to complete.

1. **Getting Face-To-Face** – The culmination of your initial prospecting efforts with the HNW individual you have targeted is to schedule your first face-to-face meeting. Asking for that meeting was a type of mini-close. So was any request for an introduction or referral to that person.

2. **Helping Them Know You, Like You, and Trust You** – Scheduling each subsequent meeting with them required you to make another mini-close.

3. **Building Professional Respect** – Asking permission to question a HNW prospect about a *Financial Impact Point*, an *Area of Dissatisfaction*, or their finances in general, and then asking if you could take notes were all types of mini-closes.

It is important to recognize the strategy behind building a sequence of mini-closes into your HNW Selling process. Picture *Prospect* on one end of a continuum and *Client* at the other end. Then close your eyes and imagine your HNW prospect moving away from *Prospect* and closer toward *Client* with each successful mini-close. When you close and he or she accepts, that commitment toward becoming your *Client* deepens. The deeper the commitment made along the way, the easier it will be to ultimately *Clinch the Relationship* at the end.

WHEN To Ask, WHAT To Ask, and HOW To Ask It

Probably the best time to *Clinch the Relationship* is at the point described at the end of the Chapter 9:

- You used reverse psychology to explain your selectivity in selecting HNW clients.

- With their permission, you used your *Promotional Piece* to show them how you would work with them, and how that would benefit them.

- You used your *Financial Organizer* as tangible evidence of how your Financial Advisory Process would address their needs.

The answer to the **"WHEN should I ask?"** question should come during the time you are using your *Promotional Piece* and *Financial Organizer* to explain your Financial Advisory Process, and they are signaling that they are ready to buy. How will you know they are ready? Look and listen for these **buying signals**.

- They nod in agreement and give positive responses.

- They lean their body forward, and their tone of voice becomes relaxed.

- They express a strong preference when you present alternative solutions and ask them which they prefer.

- Their questions switch to such things as cost, when can you start, and how long various stages of your Financial Advisory Process will take.

- They make a strong verbal commitment, such as "Sounds good," to the things you say.

- They make a negative/positive statement such as, "Of course I wouldn't be able to start this process until we get back from Europe."

- They reach for your *Promotional Piece* or *Financial Organizer*, ask to look at it, and start making positive comments or asking questions about specific items.

- They ask for assurance with questions like, "That's interesting. Which do you think would be best?"

- They comment on how they will feel being involved with you, such as "It will sure be good to have all my documents in a *Financial Organizer.*"

WHAT to ask is also very important.

Jerry was one of two senior partners in a team transitioning into the arena of wealth management. They were part of an "Achievers Group" who met quarterly to focus on building a 21st Century Financial Practice. Armed with a Financial Organizer, a new presentation folder, and his newly developed Financial Advisory Process (which he had been role playing with his partner), he met with one of their key centers-of-influence. His goal was to re-position his team and test how well these changes would be accepted by this very powerful attorney.

"I hadn't gotten to the third step in our Financial Advisory Process," explained Jerry, "I was using the presentation folder (quite proud of what we had created) when I was interrupted and

asked, 'Now that you're doing all of this, what is your minimum account size going to be?'"

Not having established a minimum account size, but wanting to attract HNW clients with at least one million dollars in investable assets, Jerry mumbled, "Well, uh, we're trying to keep it some-where in the neighborhood of one million dollars." Whew! As he told this story, I could almost see the sweat dripping off his brow.

The attorney's response was insightful: "I didn't think you could handle anything less than one million and still provide all these services. I don't know anyone around here who is taking this comprehensive approach to managing their clients' financial affairs. I will be able to send you a lot of business. I was going to give you a referral today, but they only have 450 thousand dol-lars, and I don't want to bog you down."

As we discussed this in the group, I asked Jerry what he was thinking as he was driving away from that meeting. "I wish I had that 450 thousand dollar account," was his response. Then he smiled and continued. "But I realize if I hadn't mentioned one million dollars, this attorney likely would not have provided the tremendous referrals we have come to expect from him."

Jerry was no rookie financial advisor. Along with his partner, they man-aged in excess of 460 million dollars and produced over three million dol-lars annually. Their new, exclusive focus on HNW prospects required them to make some very specific changes. To their credit, they found the courage to stay with their plan.

There are three things to which a HNW prospect must agree, and all three must be "closed" before you can conclude that you have clinched the rela-tionship:

- **Acceptance of your Financial Advisory Process** with the solu-tions, documents, etc. that will evolve from that process.

- **Willingness to transfer assets to your management**, in the amount which matches or exceeds your minimum investable asset requirement.

- **Acceptance of your fee structure**, both in terms of how you will earn your fees and/or commissions, and what they can expect to actually pay for your services.

How to close those three items and clinch the relationship is a matter of choice. The **five closing techniques** described below provide some options. Keep in mind that you need to close on each of the three items above – either individually, or all at once.

1. **The Succession Close**. This method requires a series of decisions, starting with already acceptable points, and ending with the asset transfer and fee structure decisions. It is based on the idea that once your HNW prospect has said "yes" several times, they should be ready to say "yes" to those two final decisions. Your task is to use questions to solicit those decisions, as illustrated by these examples.

   - *It seems that creating a valuation report of your business should be done as soon as possible, wouldn't you agree?*

   - *It's also important to get a better handle on the tax implications of this sale, don't you think?*

   - *You would also like help with determining how to temporarily diversify the investment of your initial lump-sum payment, isn't that true?*

   By soliciting a "yes" and writing each item down, you are confirming your readiness to give them the help they need and want. Then, you will be ready to continue.

   - *It appears we would be managing about $8.5 million for you. Are there any other assets you would like us to include at this time?*

   - *Our fee structure for working with you would be (you fill in), which is pretty standard in our community for this level of assets. Is that acceptable to you?*

   The final "yes" should clinch the relationship, but you don't want to assume anything. So, you have one final question.

   - *It sounds like you are ready to have us work with you. Shall we meet next Wednesday morning, say around 10 A.M., or would you like to begin sooner?*

A "yes" response means you have sealed the deal. Congratulations! End by saying …

- *Here is a list of documents we would like you to bring to our next meeting.*

2. **The Assumptive Close**. This approach is best used when you can safely assume they're ready to clinch the relationship. You actually begin where the Succession Close ends.

- *It sounds like you are ready to have us work with you. Shall we meet next Wednesday morning, say around 10 A.M., or would you like to begin sooner?*

A "yes" response in this case, however, does not close the deal. You still need to confirm the other two parts of this deal, but you're safely assuming they will accept both. So you simply, say …

- *It appears we would be managing about $8.5 million for you. Are there any other assets you would like us to include at this time?*

- *Our fee structure for working with you would be* (you fill in), *which is pretty standard in our community for this level of assets. Is that acceptable to you?*

A "yes" response (with possible additional assets heading your way!) does indeed clinch the relationship. End by saying the following...

- *Here is a list of documents we would like you to bring to our next meeting.*

3. **The Testimonial Close**. You can use this close when you feel they need one last reassurance that you, and your Financial Advisory Process, will meet their needs. Go back to the story of evidence you used, tell them how you started working with that person, and tell them they can expect the same. It goes something like this.

- *You remember when I described how we* (brief summary of the solution)? *We began working with them on a Wednesday in July and* (describe the first couple of advisory steps and how they enabled you to achieve that solution). *I can see a similar result in working with you. If you're ready to start, we can meet this Friday, say at 9 A.M., or would next Monday at 9 be better?*

Again, you still have to confirm the other two parts of the relationship, which you can do by following the Assumptive Close example. End by saying this...

- *Here is a list of documents we would like you to bring to our next meeting.*

4. **The Solution Close**. This close is designed to strengthen their professional respect for you so they will be ready to decide. You go back to the *Financial Impact Point* or *Area of Dissatisfaction* and use it to build their desire to immediately have the solutions you can provide. It goes something like this ...

- *We talked at length about* (state what the focus was). *From our discussion, I believe we can help you* (describe the solutions they can expect). *The sooner we get started the better. Shall we meet this Friday, say at 9 A.M., or would next Monday at 9 be better?*

Of course, you still have to confirm the other two parts of the relationship, which again you can do by following the Assumptive Close example. End by saying ...

- *Here is a list of the documents we would like you to bring to that meeting.*

5. **The Straightforward Close**. When you believe they know you, like you, trust you, and professionally respect you enough to be ready to clinch the relationship, go for it. This is the easiest approach. If they have any objections or reservations, this approach will quickly bring them to the surface. There are three questions you need to ask.

- (Name*), I feel this is a good fit, I want very much to work with you. I hope you feel the same. Are you ready to schedule the next step?*

- *It appears we would be managing about $8.5 million for you. Are there any other assets you would like us to include at this time?*

- *Our fee structure for working with you would be* (you fill in), *which is pretty standard in our community for this level of assets. Is that acceptable to you?*

This assumes, of course, that they will respond positively to each question. If they do, schedule the next meeting. Then you have clinched the relationship. End by saying …

- *Here is a list of documents we would like you to bring to our next meeting.*

But, what if a HNW prospect **raises objections or stalls**? If they do, it will almost always be one of the four responses described below. The first three are objections, at least on the surface. The last one is a definite stall. Any of these four could surface with any of the above close attempts. If it happens, smile and say you understand. Then ask, "Do you mind if I ask you a few questions?" If they say it's OK to ask, then use the questions and responses under each of the objections and stalls described below.

I'm satisfied with my advisor (broker, financial planner, etc.)?

1. Questions:

- *How long have you been with this advisor (broker, financial planner, etc.)?*

- *How did your relationship begin?*

- *What are the things you like best about working with this advisor (broker, etc.)?*

- *What would you change if you could?*

If they give you straight answers, then here's how you can respond.

Response:

- Explain how your Financial Advisory Process and expertise will 1) match what the prospect likes best about their present advisor, and 2) correct what they would like to change.

- Ask if there are any other issues. If so, address them. If not …

- Ask if you can suggest a next step.

- If you can legitimately do so, also explain how several of your select clientele had at least one or more relationships they left when they came with you – and that you will make this a simple and painless process.

Your next step is to select the appropriate Closing Method and try again.

If they won't give you straight answers and you sense it's simply a stall, use one of the three questions under item 4 below to try to discover the problem.

2. **I want to check with one or two other advisors first.**

Questions:

- *Have you determined when you will be doing this?*
- *Do you have a deadline for your decision?*
- *Can you tell me the most important things you will be checking and comparing?*

If they give you straight answers, then here's how you can respond.

- If the "most important things" include anything you haven't addressed thus far, ask permission to go over them now.
- Ask if there are any other issues. If so, address them. If not ...
- Ask if they still want to check with other advisors – or if they are satisfied with what you've discussed with them and are ready to proceed to the next step.
- Encourage them to be as careful and selective as you have suggested they be with you.

If they still want to talk with other advisors, ask if you could contact them again afterwards – and if you can, schedule a contact date with them.

If they won't give you straight answers and you sense it's simply a stall, use one of the three questions under item 4 below to try to discover the problem.

3. **Your fees are too high.**

Questions:

- *Is there anything about our fee structure that isn't clear?*
- *Could you tell me what you are comparing our fees to?*
- *If I could bring our fees more in line with what you are expecting, would you reconsider?* (ask only if you believe you can re-quote fees that they may accept).

If they give you straight answers, then here's how you can respond.

Response:

- Explain how your fees are determined and exactly what they receive for those fees. Then explain the adjustments (if any) you are willing to make.
- Ask if there are any other issues. If so, address them. If not ...
- Ask if you can proceed to the next step.

Your next step is to select the appropriate Closing Method and try again.

If they won't give you straight answers and you sense it's simply a stall, use one of the three questions under item 4 below to try to discover the problem.

4. **I want to think about it.**

    This is not an objection; **it's a stall**. There's a problem. Use one of the three questions below to try to open a dialog to discover what's wrong.

    If they resisted your questions with any of the above objections or stalls, then there's **a problem you probably aren't aware of**. You won't find out what is wrong unless you ask. Here are questions you can use:

    - *Are there some other issues that need to be resolved first?*
    - *Would you mind telling me what's wrong with what I've suggested?*
    - *Have I offended you in any way with my suggestion?*

You are using these questions to try to begin a dialog that will take you to the heart of the issue. If something is truly wrong, you cannot advance the sale in any way until it is resolved.

What They Need for You to Clinch the Relationship

You are convinced they know you, like you, trust you, and have enough professional respect for you that they are ready to clinch the relationship. That's the level of confidence that moving through the *HNW Selling*

Process gives you. When you attempted to close the deal and they said "yes," it was because you did the following …

- Successfully performed a series of mini-closes, beginning in the initial face-to-face meeting and continuing right up to this point.
- Knew exactly what to ask, and when to ask it.
- Selected wisely from five closing techniques because you knew when and how to use each effectively.
- Overcame any objections or stalls effectively.

In Chapter 9, you met Jack and learned how he repositioned himself with 15 existing HNW clients. What I didn't tell you was that an under-achieving veteran in his branch had been watching Jack's success. He had a physician friend that he had always been afraid to prospect, so he finally asked Jack to teach him what he was doing.

> *One afternoon after the market closed, Jack spent about 45 minutes walking his colleague through his newly developed Financial Advisory Process, his Financial Organizer, and the verbiage he had been using. They role-played, and he armed his associate with one of his Financial Organizers.*

> *The following afternoon, this underachieving but newly trained financial advisor met with his physician friend. He not only clinched the relationship, but was asked by his friend if he would present his services to the remaining 44 physicians who worked in his medical group. Over time, this former underachiever clinched the relationship with all 45 physicians. Later, this medical practice merged with another 20 physician practice. He now has 65 physicians who look to him as their go-to financial quarterback.*

Make no mistake about it. If this underachieving veteran could do a complete 360 in his attitude, master the *HNW Selling Process* to the extent he was able to close 65 physicians as their go-to financial quarterback, the HNW world is out there for any financial professional brave enough to go for it. It took tremendous courage for this plateaued advisor to ask for help and then meet with his physician friend.

To make certain you approach this phase with both courage and skill, here's a list of do's and don'ts from this chapter to keep key points fresh in your memory:

Do	Don't
Confirm the "yes" for each mini-close; from prospecting through building profess-ional respect.	Assume "yes" for each mini-close and later discover you have unresolved problems.
Be aware throughout your presentation of your Finan-cial Advisory Process to determine the right time to ask (close).	Forget the importance of closing the sale and finish your presenta-tion by simply thanking them for their time and attention.
Close the acceptance of your Financial Advisory Process plus your minimum asset level and fee structure.	Assume that acceptance of your Financial Advisory Process auto-matically means acceptance of the other two areas.
Master all 5 closing techn-iques so you can use them wisely.	Assume that one close fits all.
Be prepared to handle all 4 objections and stalls.	Let an objection or stall throw you for any reason.
Finalize your close with a specific date and time to be-gin the working relationship.	Say, "I'll call you later to see if we can get together some time."

Managing the
HNW Client
Relationship

Chapter 11
Delivering What You Promised

Chapter 12
Staying on Your Critical Path to Success

11

Delivering What You Promised

You are now initiating the **I Will Conduct Business With You** opportunity you created by following the Critical Path and skillfully performing the *HNW Selling Process*. You implement the opportunity through a series of working meetings — with you and your client each carrying out defined responsibilities between those meetings. Your success will ultimately lead to the **I'll Refer You** benefit that results from effectively delivering what you sold.

We live in a *Try Before You Buy* and *Unconditional Money-Back Guarantee* age. The Internet has had considerable influence in creating that expectation by allowing instant download of products and sign-up of services on a trial basis. That doesn't work for financial services, and you want to make certain it doesn't become an issue with your new HNW clients.

With financial services, the trial period begins after you have clinched the relationship. It is vital that your new client remain convinced that you are delivering what you sold.

Delivering What You Sold

What you promised was a Financial Advisory Process that they decided would provide the financial solutions they need. You must convince them that they made the right choice. A key element is the "managing expectations" challenge introduced in Chapter 9:

> **Managing Expectations**
>
> From the questions you ask, the answers they give, and the various things you discuss, they may develop expectations about the relationship you could easily overlook if you do not clarify them right away. Immediately after you set the first work session appointment, go over your notes and write down everything you can think of that they might be expecting you to do.

> Review and confirm the list with them at the first meeting. Then ask if there is anything else they expect from you that you have not mentioned.

In our book, *How to Build a 21st Century Financial Practice*, we outlined a six-step Financial Advisory Process. These are steps in the process, not client meetings. You need to determine which step or steps will be completed at each client meeting you schedule. Regardless of how you organize and implement these steps, there are two vital and tangible outcomes which must result from each one: *decisions* and *deliverables*. Making certain each outcome is achieved is the way you demonstrate you are truly delivering what you promised.

To make this more practical for you, we have organized the steps into a series of *working meetings*. Following are the steps to be completed, plus the key decisions and deliverables for each meeting. You will need to adjust this list to your needs, and even more important, to the needs and desires of each client.

Think back to Chapter 10 when the attorney said to Jerry, *"I didn't think you could handle anything less than one million and still provide all these services."* As you go though the following working meetings, the wisdom of the "provide all those services" statements will become even more clear.

1. **Working Meeting #1**

   For this meeting, you ask your HNW client to gather and bring all his or her financial records and documents (see each close described in Chapter 10). Give the client a checklist of documents to bring to the first meeting so he or she will know what is expected.

   STEPS To Be Completed:

   - Step 1: Establish and define the client-advisor relationship.

   - Step 2: Gather client data, including goals and risk tolerance.

   Key DECISIONS:

   - The client's lifestyle and financial needs, priorities, and goals.

   - The client's time frame for specific desired results.

   - The client's risk tolerance and how that tempers each expectation.

- Your responsibilities, and your client's responsibilities for making this process successful.

- How decisions will be made. This could range from you simply running decisions by them for approval to presenting alternatives from which they will choose. Keep in mind that the research shows that HNW investors are typically confident in their ability to make good decisions. What they want from a go-to financial advisor is not "what to do," but the information and options that will enable them to make those decisions.

- When you will meet next, the objectives and a tentative agenda for that meeting, and what each of you will do in preparation for that meeting.

Key DELIVERABLES:

- A written report detailing the decisions made at the meeting – delivered within ___ working days. This number should become a standard, not a number that changes depending on how you feel. "Two working days" is a good benchmark.

2. **Working Meeting #2**

   STEPS To Be Completed:

   - Step 3: Analyze and evaluate the client's financial status.

   - Step 4: Develop and present financial planning recommendations and/or alternatives (Financial Plan).

   Key DECISIONS:

   - Client choices relating to recommendations and alternatives presented as part of the draft of their Financial Plan.

   - Your responsibilities, and your client's responsibilities for making this Financial Plan successful.

   - The problem areas and opportunities that need to be addressed.

   - Which financial records and documents to include in their *Financial Organizer.*

   - When you will meet next, the objectives and a tentative agenda for that meeting, and what each of you will do to prepare.

Key DELIVERABLES:

- Their *Financial Organizer* with all selected financial records and documents inserted.

- The finalized Financial Plan – delivered on or before the date set during the meeting. Depending on the circumstances, you may want to schedule another meeting to deliver and go over the Plan, especially if significant changes were made from the draft.

- A written report detailing the decisions made at the meeting – delivered within ___ working days.

3. **Ongoing Working Meetings**

   STEPS To Be Completed:

   - Step 5: Implement the financial planning recommendations.

   - Step 6: Monitor the financial planning recommendations.

   Key DECISIONS:

   - What you will do to implement and monitor the plan, and what you will do to keep the client fully advised.

   - What the client will do to implement the plan, and what you will do to coach him or her.

   - Milestone events that will determine the need for you to contact the client, address the issue, and possibly schedule a *Working Meeting*. Examples are: changes in tax laws, economic circumstances, or changes in the client's personal or financial status.

   - A schedule for Quarterly Update meetings, or whatever time frame you choose.

   - For each *Working Meeting* — when you will meet next, the objectives and a tentative agenda for that meeting, and what each of you will do in preparation for that meeting.

   Key DELIVERABLES:

   - Updates for the client's Financial Plan.

   - Updates for the client's *Financial Organizer*.

   - Written reports on investments and changes to any financial documents.

- For each *Working Meeting* – a written report detailing the decisions made at the meeting – delivered within ___ working days.

Obviously, the number and sequence of these meetings will be decided by both you and your HNW client. Whenever you can condense the process, by all means, do so. I recall a motivated HNW prospect who was referred to a financial advisor by his CPA and came armed with every piece of financial information he could lay his hands on. There was very little this financial advisor could do to blow the deal. Well, not really. He could stall the close, which is precisely what this advisor did. Somewhat shocked by the eagerness of this HNW prospect, his sad attempt at a mini-close was to suggest this HNW prospect take a few days to think about everything they discussed. Because of schedules, it took another nine weeks for this relationship to be consummated. Ouch! He should have clinched the relationship right then and there.

Dealing With The "How Am I Doing?" Client

You may discover you have a client who constantly "peeks" at his or her investments, possibly on a daily basis. You know the problems this creates. How should you respond?

There is a unique area of psychology called Behavioral Economics, that provides helpful insight into the issues involved. As you know, dissatisfaction is a major reason why affluent investors are willing to consider switching to a new advisor. It is an important part of building professional respect that we discussed in Chapter 9. As pointed out by Nassim Nicholas Taleb in his book, *Fooled by Randomness*, the more often your new clients "peek" at their investments, the more likely they are to be dissatisfied with the results.

Assume this investment portfolio:

- An expected rate of return of 15% with annual returns varying by 10% from this average.

According to Taleb, if they look at their investments each day, there's a 46% probability they will discover they have lost money. Look at what happens in other time frames:

- Checking monthly – a 33% chance they will have lost money.

- Checking quarterly – a 23% chance they will have lost money

- Checking yearly – a 7% chance they will have lost money

Not only does constant "peeking" provide a distorted view of their portfolio, psychologists say the pain of loss is felt 2 to 2.5 times more deeply than the thrill of an equivalent gain. Short-term thinking significantly increases the probability of becoming dissatisfied.

Encourage your HNW client to keep their focus on quarterly reviews, or even monthly reviews, if they are impatient. From our above example portfolio, there is a 77% probability they will have made money when you conduct a Quarterly Review; a 65% probability if you conduct a Monthly Review.

If they do keep "peeking," explain how easily they can become fooled by random checking. Using the above example, there's about an equal probability they could find either a gain or loss each time they look. For help with making calculations for your clients' portfolios, see *Fooled by Randomness: The Hidden Role of Chance in the Markets and in Life* by Nassim Nicholas Taleb (Texere, 2001).

If They Concur, They Will Refer

The emerging field of Customer Relationship Management has taught us some important lessons. For one, we know that the cost of landing a new client is about five times the cost of maintaining the loyalty of an existing one.

We have also discovered that a satisfied client is not the same as a loyal client. Satisfaction is a fleeting emotion which results from the last transaction you had with them, and is not a promise they will buy from you again. In fact, your quick and effective response to client dissatisfaction actually helps to build client loyalty.

The **I'll Refer You** benefit evolves from behaviors you repeat over and over. It's the result of the highly valued relationship you've worked hard to build. A loyal client can be expected to do four things:

- Use your services in the future.
- Eagerly consider new strategies, products, and services you offer.
- Resist the "pull" from competitors.
- Provide solicited and unsolicited referrals.

The important message here is that because they concur with what you are doing, they will refer new prospects to you. Your efforts to manage client relationships and build client loyalty will enable you to quickly build your business exclusively on referrals. Loyal clients will contribute in three ways:

1. They will send friends, business associates, and even people they meet to you — unsolicited.

2. They will agree to act as an Internal Advocate to their circles of influence – social and business related. They will invite you to the right functions, and provide the most powerful type of connection you could ever want — a personal introduction.

3. When asked, they will provide the names of friends, business associates, and acquaintances. They may even agree to contact those individuals and let them know you will be calling.

They absolutely will refer, especially if you ask. If you have any doubts, go back and review the examples used throughout this book. Each is true, and most include referrals which resulted from the good efforts to meet the needs of a HNW prospect or client.

What They Need to Continue Doing Business With You

After clinching the relationship, you immediately begin a series of *Working Meetings* to make certain that you meet their expectations and deliver what you sold. What you sold, of course, was yourself — backed by your Financial Advisory Process. The *Working Meetings* are the tangible expression of that process.

Your efforts are not simply to deliver services, but to also build client loyalty. Each HNW client's response in exhibiting the loyalty behaviors listed above evolve because you do the following:

- Establish objectives and an agenda for each *Working Meeting*.

- Cover the agenda items and documented key decisions at each *Working Meeting*.

- Define at the end of each *Working Meeting* when you will meet next, the objectives and tentative agenda for the next meeting, and what each of you will do to prepare.

- Provide a written report of the decisions made at each meeting – and deliver it within two working days.

- Provide your client with a comprehensive Financial Plan.

- Keep the client's *Financial Organizer* up-to-date.

- Respond to needs quickly and effectively.

To ensure that your HNW clients will continue doing business with you, here is a list of do's and don'ts from this chapter to keep key points fresh in your memory:

Do	Don't
Make a list of client expectations immediately after you clinch the relationship – and before your first Working Meeting.	Put off listing client expectations – or not do it at all, assuming you'll remember.
Give the client a checklist of financial records and documents they should bring to your first Working Meeting.	Simply tell them to bring the financial records and documents to the first Working Meeting, later to discover something important is missing.
Write down key decisions as they are made at each Working Meeting.	Wait until the end of the meeting to write down key decisions and risk not remembering them.
Set objectives and a tentative agenda for the next meeting at the end of each Working Meeting.	Create an agenda just before the next meeting, if at all.
Deliver a written report of each Working Meeting within 2 working days.	Delay, or forget to send a written report.

Do	Don't
Do what you can to discourage clients from frequent "peeking" to see how their investments are doing. Deal with it if they do.	Ignore their disappointments if they do "peek" often.
Track loyalty building behaviors and solicit introductions and referrals as soon and as often as appropriate.	Focus on simply keeping clients satisfied.

12

Staying on Your Critical Path to Success

As you read through the first 11 chapters, you may have felt a bit overwhelmed at times. That's only natural. Many of the techniques presented in this book may be familiar, but the *HNW Selling Process* has placed them in a new and challenging context. You probably want to know how to apply these techniques quickly and effectively.

Whatever you presently do every day, whether you believe it's effective or not, you do out of habit. Experts tell us that 80% of our behavior is "habit driven." *Mental habits* stored in our subconscious mind shape and drive our attitudes. *Doing habits*, also stored there, emerge as behavioral patterns which shape and drive our actions. Over time, what we repeatedly think and do becomes comfortable. It's what we often refer to as our *comfort zone*. Breaking out of your Comfort Zone and developing new attitudes and behavioral patterns is the key to mastering the inner challenges related to achieving HNW Selling success.

Becoming a Go-To HNW Financial Quarterback

In Chapter 3, we emphasized that the **Go-To HNW Financial Quarterback** of the 21st Century must do these eight things very well:

21st Century Go-To HNW Financial Quarterback Profile

1. Master the HNW Selling Process.
2. Be skilled in maintaining a high level of interaction with each HNW client.
3. Possess a wide breadth and depth of knowledge about the products and services offered in eight key financial areas.
4. Be reasonably conversant about each product and service, and be capable of easily explaining how each integrates with the others.

155

5. Be familiar enough with each HNW client's needs to know when to bring in a particular specialist.

6. Form strategic partner relationships with skilled specialists, and establish the right type of working agreement and compensation arrangement with each.

7. Build and manage a Financial Advisory Team made up of staff and strategic partners, and keep them focused on serving HNW clients.

8. Keep up with ongoing financial product and service developments, and be familiar enough with your HNW client needs to know what to add and when to make the recommendation.

On the first page of Chapter 1, we established the importance of mastering HNW Selling with this statement.

Mastering HNW Selling is your Critical Path to building a successful 21st Century Financial Practice

I'd like to review and summarize exactly what that means and what needs to happen.

- The *Critical Path* concept defines what needs to be your highest priority activity each day.

- HNW Selling is the core of your Critical Path. That is what must dominate your daily thinking and activity. Everything else is secondary.

- Following your Critical Path is what will propel you toward becoming a go-to HNW financial quarterback. Your Critical Path focuses on mastering the HNW Selling Process and maintaining interaction with each HNW client, which are the first two parts of the above profile. By following your Critical Path each day, other aspects of that profile will be drawn into your daily activity at the right time and in the right way.

- As you focus on your Critical Path (HNW Selling), you will find both the need and opportunity to delegate other important activities to other members of your team.

- As you evolve into an effective go-to HNW financial quarterback as defined by the profile, you will successfully build a 21st Century Financial Practice.

It is easy to become distracted. I have seen financial advisors commit to building a 21st Century Financial Practice and then spend the first six months forming a team, creating a new promotional brochure, and getting ready to perform all the other tasks related to servicing HNW clients. The problem is that because they kept wandering off their Critical Path, they didn't have any new HNW clients to serve.

Here's an example of how one wise financial advisor avoided this trap.

Bert was determined to do whatever it took to build a successful 21st Century Financial Practice. A retail business owner in his previous life, Bert was used to multi-tasking. He believed that ability would see him through as he began to systematically tackle all the tasks and activities detailed in the kit.

We had talked about the Critical Path concept, and Bert knew that activities which would place him face-to-face with HNW clients, HNW upgrade clients, HNW prospects, and centers-of-influence were his top priority. How could he do all this plus accomplish all the other tasks related to transforming his practice? As he pondered this question, he realized that doing all those other tasks were more comfortable for him than doing what was required to arrange those face-to-face encounters. Focus, not multi-tasking, was the solution.

The next day, Bert began delegating everything except his Top 25 Referral & Master Dream List notebook and Critical Path fixed daily activities. Within the first week Bert was able to orchestrate four key HNW face-to-face contacts, get three quality introductions, and place six million dollars into his pipeline.

His staff was still working on his Financial Organizer and Presentation Folder, and he had yet to complete the segmentation of his entire client base. Nevertheless, he was already journeying down his Critical Path and beginning to master the HNW

Selling Process. An interesting aside was a comment he made during week two. "Matt, I'm following the exact verbiage we discussed for generating introductions. It's really quite simple. Not only does it work, but the HNW people I used it with were anxious to help. Ironically, our firm just sent us a piece on how to ask for referrals, and they are telling us to do precisely what you say not to do."

Staying with your Critical Path is what enables you to develop the skills to perform Critical Path activities the right way. Let's say you start asking for introductions and are not experiencing success. In order to stay on your Critical Path, you will find a way to learn the necessary skills and make adjustments. The Critical Path method requires that you not only perform the requisite HNW Selling activities, but that you perform them well. Taking a break from those activities is not an option.

The difference between so many financial advisors and Bert is in applying the Critical Path concept to their prioritization of activities. Whereas Bert began immediately working on his HNW Selling skills and getting face-to-face with HNW clients and prospects, other financial advisors will allow themselves to become distracted from their HNW sales activities. The Critical Path Method is your best weapon agains avoidance traps.

Paving The Critical Path With Fixed Daily Activities

When you initially step onto your Critical Path, you are faced with one other reality: your *day job*. In the beginning, your Critical Path needs to include a constantly shifting blend of day job and HNW Selling activities.

- Your day job includes activities necessary to maintain what you now have so you can continue to "make a living." As soon as you bring in additional or new HNW assets, those activities begin to fade into the past.

- HNW Selling activities bring you ever closer to the go-to HNW financial quarterback profile. As your day job activity fades, these activities take over.

The key to making that happen is to be certain all that activity is *focused activity*. This is where Fixed Daily Activities (FDAs) enter the picture.

Without focused activity, we tend to spend our day basically *reacting* to whatever happens. Defining Fixed Daily Activities enable us to become *proactive* about everything we do because everything has a purpose.

- *Fixed* means we have determined and committed to those activities in advance.
- *Daily* means we are doing fixed activities each day, even though the specific activities may change from day to day.
- *Activities* have a clear purpose and are linked to important goals.

The completion of each Fixed Daily Activity brings you one step closer to the future you greatly desire.

Fixed Daily Activities will help you deal with the realities of maintaining your *day job* for a time, while successfully building a *21st Century Financial Practice* targeting HNW clients.

A Critical Path of HNW Sales & Marketing Success form has been developed to facilitate the process. This form is illustrated in Figures 12-1, 12-2, 12-3, and 12-4.

- Weekly Activity ORGANIZER (Fig. 12-1)   page 160
- Weekly Activity SCHEDULER (Fig. 12-2)   page 161
- Weekly Activity SCHEDULER, Part 2 (Fig. 12-3)   page 162
- Pipeline TRACKING and Weekly Metrics   page 163
  SCORECARD (Fig. 12-4)

You can download a free PDF file of this form which can be reviewed and printed in Adobe Acrobat Reader.

Go to: http://www.oechsli.com/cpform.html

Figure 12-1: Weekly Activity ORGANIZER … to help you plan your week.

Critical Path ORGANIZER   Week of __/__/__ to __/__/__

Face-To-Face Contacts
Activity Drives The Dream!   Type of Contact   Type of Contact

Client Review Meetings   **Objective: Retain Key Clients**

Client Upgrade Meetings   **Objective: Gain Additional Assets**

Client Networking   **Objective: Arrange Introductions & Referrals**

Referral Alliance Contacts   **Objective: Arrange Introductions & Referrals**

HNW Prospect – Introductions   **Objective: Bring into My Pipeline**

HNW Prospect – Referral Contacts   **Objective: Bring into My Pipeline**

HNW Prospect – Placing Myself in their Path   **Objective: Bring into My Pipeline**

Type of Contact: P = Phone Call   E = Email   M = Scheduled Meeting   S = Social Event

Your Critical Path to HNW Selling Success

Figure 12-2: Weekly Activity SCHEDULER, Part 1 … to help you plan each day.

Weekly Activity SCHEDULER

Monday _____	Tuesday _____	Wednesday _____	Thursday _____
7 _____	7 _____	7 _____	7 _____
8 _____	8 _____	8 _____	8 _____
9 _____	9 _____	9 _____	9 _____
10 _____	10 _____	10 _____	10 _____
11 _____	11 _____	11 _____	11 _____
12 _____	12 _____	12 _____	12 _____
1 _____	1 _____	1 _____	1 _____
2 _____	2 _____	2 _____	2 _____
3 _____	3 _____	3 _____	3 _____
4 _____	4 _____	4 _____	4 _____
5 _____	5 _____	5 _____	5 _____
6 _____	6 _____	6 _____	6 _____
7 _____	7 _____	7 _____	7 _____
8 _____	8 _____	8 _____	8 _____
9 _____	9 _____	9 _____	9 _____
Phone/email/fax: ✓	Phone/email/fax: ✓	Phone/email/fax: ✓	Phone/email/fax: ✓

Figure 12-3: Weekly Activity SCHEDULER, Part 2 … to help you plan each day and schedule other activities.

		Other Activities TO SCHEDULE ✓
Friday _____	Saturday _____	**Day Job Activities**
7 _____		
8 _____		
9 _____		
10 _____		
11 _____		
12 _____		
1 _____		**Business Builder Activities**
2 _____		
3 _____		
4 _____	Sunday _____	
5 _____		
6 _____		
7 _____		
8 _____		
9 _____		**Family & Health Activities**
Phone/email/fax: ✓	Phone/email/fax: ✓	

Figure 12-4: Pipleine TRACKING and Weekly Metrics SCORE-CARD ... to help you plan, measure, and analyze your weekly activity.

Pipeline TRACKING

| [1]Status: | C = Current | N = New this week |

Name	[1]Status	Asset Potential	[2]Stage of Development
1			
2			
3			
4			
5			
6			
7			
8			
9			
10			
11			
12			
13			
14			
15			
16			
17			
18			

| [2]Five Stages of Development | • First face-to-face • Building rapport/trust • Uncovering a "financial impact point" • Establishing my QB competence • Clinching the relationship |

Weekly Metrics SCORECARD

Transfer from the previous pages.

CLIENT Contacts	Target	Actual
• Client Review Meetings	___	___
• Client Upgrade Meetings	___	___
• Client Networking Contacts	___	___

REFERRAL Alliance Contacts	Target	Actual
• Referral Alliance Contacts	___	___

PROSPECT Contacts	Target	Actual
• HNW Prospect – Introductions	___	___
• HNW Prospect – Referral Contacts	___	___
• HNW Prospect Contacts – From Placing Myself in their Path	___	___

1. **Plan Your Week** — There are seven types of business development contacts. You need to make a set number of contacts of some type each day. Those types include the following:

   - Client review meetings

   - Client upgrade meetings

   - Client networking contacts

   - Referral alliance contacts

   - HNW prospect introductions

   - HNW prospect referral contacts

   - HNW prospect contacts through placing yourself in their path

   Before the week begins, use the **Weekly Activity ORGANIZER** (Fig.12-1) to list the names of people in each of the above categories that you will contact that week. Then set Targets for how many contacts you will make in each category on your **Weekly Metrics SCORECARD** (Fig. 12-4).

2. **Plan Each Day** – Each day, you should create a list of Day Job, Business Builder, Family, and Health Activities; writing each in your **Weekly Activity SCHEDULER** (Fig. 12-2 and 12-3).

   You should also meet first thing in the morning with your current support staff to review the previous day, and to preview the Fixed Daily Activities for the day. Ask if there is anything they need from you, and then make certain you provide whatever they need. This is the most effective way I know to go from being reactive to proactive.

3. **Measure Your Weekly Activity** – At the end of each week, record in your **Weekly Metrics SCORECARD** (Fig. 12-4) the actual number of contacts you made in each of the seven categories – noting where you were over or under the target you established at the beginning of the week.

4. **Analyze Your Weekly Activity** – On your **Weekly Metrics SCORECARD** (Fig. 12-4), write your thoughts about why you were over target or under target. Then include ideas of what you can do next week to improve.

Those Monday Mornin' Blues

Imagine that you spent the weekend planning the first week of your **Critical Path Sales and Marketing System**. Everything is recorded on your Organizer, Scheduler, and Scorecard. You have been puzzling all weekend over these challenges.

Now, today is Monday morning! You're thinking …

"I'm not really up to making my first HNW prospecting call this morning.

I think I will _____ instead." (You fill in the blank)

That reaction is very predictable. It's called the **Non-Achievement Cycle**. As you got closer to the moment of truth when you needed to take your first prospecting step, those negative FEELINGS about prospecting emerged. You began THINKING about what kind of excuse you could come up with as a reason to DO something else – whatever you wrote in the above blank — which was not what you should be doing!

Now that you understand what happened, the challenge is to reverse this cycle — to replace that negative feeling-thinking-doing sequence with a behavioral pattern that will enable you to achieve something, and move you closer toward your goal. Visualize this process, replacing the pattern below on the left with the pattern on the right.

Non-Achievement Cycle   **Achievement Cycle**

DOING is the key to successfully activate your *HNW Selling Process.* The Non-Achievement Cycle is replaced by DOING your Fixed Daily Activities first – regardless of what you THINK – or how you FEEL.

Go back and review Bert's story. Notice how quickly he activated his Achievement Cycle by doing what he knew he must do to move ahead, despite the fact it was somewhat uncomfortable for him to take that step.

Doing is almost completely under our control. It is how we break out of our Comfort Zone – by doing! Doing, despite setbacks, results in achievement. Achievement creates positive thinking, which causes us to feel good. Achievement, positive thinking, and good feelings are then transferred to our subconscious mind and stored for later positive reinforcement.

After observing the financial salespeople he had managed for years, Albert E. N. Gray said this to his 1940 NALU Convention audience.

> *The common denominator of success – the secret of success of every man who has ever been successful – lies in the fact that he* ***formed the habit of doing things that failures don't like to do.***

As you activate each step of your *HNW Selling Process*, you will be confronted with feelings about things you do not like to do. Remember, these are merely feelings. Mentally push those feelings aside and DO whatever it is you know you need to do. The more you do it, the better you will begin to feel about it. You will find yourself saying, "I didn't used to like doing _____, but now that I'm better at it, I find I enjoy doing it." Amazing!

Your commitment to the Critical Path Method will protect you from being sidetracked by those Monday mornin' blues. Because you now have your priorities in order, you are focused and working to improve your HNW sales skills. You are active, and you are singing a whole different tune.

As I said earlier, the 21st century financial advisors who will earn the most money, provide the best lifestyles for their families, and enjoy the highest levels of career satisfaction are going to be an elite corps who will excel in doing three things very well.

- Getting face-to-face with High Net Worth prospects.

- Selling them on establishing a long-term financial advisory relationship.

- Managing that relationship to build the level of client loyalty required to turn the relationship into an ongoing referral generator.

Make no mistake about it, mastering HNW Selling is your CRITICAL PATH to ongoing success. May you enjoy the journey every step of the way.

References

Cap Gemini Ernst & Young. *Wealth Management Strategies for the Financial Services Industry.* August 22, 2002. White paper. Cap Gemini Ernst & Young.

Carnegie, Dale. 1990. *How to Win Friends and Influence People.* New York: Pocket Books.

Dudley, George W., and Shannon L. Goodson. 1999. *The Psychology of Sales Call Reluctance.* Dallas: Behavioral Sciences Research Press, Inc.

Market Data and Research. www.hnwadvisor.com.

Merrill Lynch/Cap Gemini Ernst & Young. 2003. *World Wealth Report 2003.* Cap Gemini Ernst & Young.

Molloy, John T. 1998. *New Dress for Success.* New York: Warner Books.

———. 1996. *New Women's Dress for Success.* New York: Warner Books.

O'Brien, James J., and Fredrick L. Plotnick. 1999. *CPM in Construction Management.* New York: McGraw-Hill Publishing, 5th edition.

Prince, Russ A., Karen Maru File, and Russ Alan Prince. 1997. *Cultivating the Affluent II: Leveraging High-Net-Worth Client and Advisor Relationships.* New York: Institutional Investor.

Taleb, Nassim Nicholas. 2001. *Fooled by Randomness: The Hidden Role of Chance in the Markets and in Life.* New York: Texere.

About Matt Oechsli

Matt Oechsli is a keynote speaker, trainer, and personal coach who has been helping financial professionals take their business and personal performance to a higher level for over 20 years. Whenever you attend a Matt Oechsli program, you can be confident that the ideas and methods he brings to you are research based – action oriented – and street tested.

His current emphasis on targeting high net worth investors emerged from a 1999 independent research project which identified 14 critical areas where financial advisors were not meeting the performance expectations of their high net worth clients.

Published in March 2002, Matt Oechsli's *How to Build a 21st Century Financial Practice* reached 1,000 in sales within the first 30 days. He has authored two other best selling books, and his articles have been published in Registered Representative and numerous other financial services trade publications.

Matt lives in Greensboro, North Carolina, with his wife and three children.

Other Oechsli Institute Products

Mastering HNW selling is your *critical path* to building a successful 21st century financial practice. You also need to be prepared for the other challenges that you will encounter along the way. These products will help you do that.

Assessing Your Financial Practice
Assessing Your Wealth Management Team

Two professional assessment tools focusing on criteria drawn from our 21st Century Financial Practice model, our 2003 research on Wealth Management Teams, and our extensive experience working with Financial Advisors. You begin by determining how important each of the criteria are to your future. Next, you will assess how well you are performing in those same areas. Then by identifying the GAPS between what you determined is important and your performance, you will be able to focus your efforts toward shaping the future direction of your financial practice. Includes a CD listening guide.

How to Build a 21st Century Financial Practice: Attracting, Servicing, and Retaining Affluent Clients

This book will serve as your personal coach, patiently guiding you every step of the way toward building your own 21st Century Financial

Practice. Each chapter will take you closer to becoming what high net worth investors want: a 'go-to' HNW financial quarterback who can skillfully coordinate and advance the multidimensional aspects of their finances. It expands on *High Net Worth Selling: The Critical Path* to address all the other aspects of building a successful practice.

101 Serious Money Selling Tips

Here's a handy pocket-sized booklet that condenses HNW selling techniques and skills into an easy-to-find and quick-to-read reference booklet. Simply glancing through a few pages each day will put you in exactly the right mindset for getting face-to-face with the HNW prospects you need to keep your pipeline filled.

Creating a Successful 21st Century Financial Practice **KIT**

Includes everything you need to build a successful Financial Advisory Team for targeting high net worth investors.

- A Benchmarking self-assessment tool to help you determine what is important to you and where you want this kit to take you.
- Strategic thinking and tactical how-to exercises to take you where you want to go.
- A *Game Plan* to guide you every step of the way.
- *Your Financial Advisory Team Guidelines* which covers all aspects of building a Wealth Management Team.

Your Financial Advisory Team Guidelines

Includes a team self-assessment tool, guidelines for organizing your team, the 12 commandments of successful teams, common pitfalls teams must avoid, tips for conducting effective team meetings, a template for developing a Team Agreement (not a legal document), and guidelines for developing a team compensation agreement that is both fair and motivational. This is the same set of team guidelines included in the KIT.